"And Then Dan Said
to Michael..."
    All The best,
        Dn Wade

"And Then Jack Said to Arnie..."

·

DON WADE

CONTEMPORARY
BOOKS
CHICAGO

Library of Congress Cataloging-in-Publication Data

Wade, Don.
    "And then Jack said to Arnie—" : A collection of the
greatest true golf stories of all time / Don Wade ;
[foreword by Lee Trevino].
       p.   cm.
    Includes index.
    ISBN 0-8092-4054-8 : $16.95
    1. Golf—Anecdotes.   2. Golf—Humor.   I. Title.
GV967.W26   1991
796.352'0207—dc20   91-6911
                                            CIP

Published by Contemporary Books, Inc.
180 North Michigan Avenue, Chicago, Illinois 60601
Manufactured in the United States of America
International Standard Book Number: 0-8092-4054-8

For the Gang of Wade, who aren't quite sure what all this golf writing business is about but do know it produces a lot of wonderful presents from the assorted Pebble Beaches and St. Andrewses of the world and, therefore, can't be all bad—or even be a real job.

CONTENTS

ACKNOWLEDGMENTS

*A*ny book is by definition a group effort, and that's certainly true in a case such as this.

The idea for doing this book grew out of a dinner conversation during the 1989 Ryder Cup at the Belfry in England, where I was doing the telecast back to the States. I was with Bob Rosen and Craig Foster, the men in charge of what is laughingly referred to as my television career. After I told them a couple of stories, Bob suggested doing this book, and off we went.

Chris Tomasino, who works with Bob and Craig and handles the literary side of the business, took over from there and did what she does so well—a combination of cheerleading, hand-holding, ego boosting, reality therapy, and negotiating. She also brought to bear her sense of humor and editing touch, which are extraordinary, and her knowledge of golf, which isn't—yet.

Lee Trevino was gracious enough to take time out from the zillion other demands on his time to do the Foreword, and his generosity is much appreciated—as is his friendship.

The same is true for Paul Szep, who paused in his Pulitzer Prize-winning bashing of politicians for the *Boston Globe* to do the illustrations. I once asked Sam Snead what he'd have been if he hadn't been a golfer. "I used to think I'd like to draw political cartoons for a paper because you'd only have to come up with one good idea a day," said Sam. "But then I realized that if I became a sportswriter I wouldn't have to come up with any."

I guess that means Szeppy and I are on the right track.

Everyone at *Golf Digest* has been terrific with stories and suggestions, and their generosity and friendship are greatly appreciated. The same is true for all the other writers, TV people, players, and general hang-around guys who helped out and who make covering golf such an absurdly pleasurable way to make a living.

And last, but by no means least, thanks to Nancy Crossman, my editor at Contemporary Books, who is what every writer needs most—a friend who truly believes.

FOREWORD

*U*ntil I was asked to write the foreword for Don Wade's
And Then Jack Said to Arnie . . . I had never really
thought about why there are so many great golf stories. I
mean, a lot of people play tennis, but when was the last
time you heard a decent tennis story?

Golf is a game that gives you a lot of time to talk. You
stand around on the tee waiting to hit your drive, you
walk to your ball, and after your round you trade lies over
a few beers. No wonder there're so many great stories
about golf.

But I think there's more to it than just that. Golf is the
most human game of them all. You have tremendous
highs and the worst lows—sometimes in the same round.
The game isn't fair, but then life isn't always fair either.
You get your share of bad bounces and good luck in both.
Maybe that's why golf fans can relate so well to the pros.
They can't hit the ball as far or putt as well, but they've
been through the same good times and bad times on the
course.

When you read about old Ky Laffoon trying to drown
his putter or Tommy Bolt running out of clubs, it's funny
as hell. But there've been a lot of times I've wanted to
strangle a club or two of my own. How about you?

I've probably gone toe to toe with Jack Nicklaus as
often as any player alive, and I thought I knew the man

pretty well. But when I read his son Jackie's wonderful story about caddying for his father, I saw a side of Jack I'd never seen before.

Bob Jones once said that there's no courage involved in golf because there's no physical danger. That may be true, but when you read the stories about Jones, or Babe Zaharias, or Ken Venturi's comeback to win the 1964 U.S. Open, you'll get crystal-clear insight into courage in its purest form.

Don has done a great job with this book. He's captured the flavor of the game and the people who play it. Reading this book is like being in a locker room with the greatest players and storytellers in golf history. So sit back and enjoy it. *And Then Jack Said to Arnie* . . . won't cure your slice, but it sure as hell will bring a smile to your face . . . and maybe a tear to your eye.

Lee Trevino

PREFACE

*T*he late British journalist Henry Longhurst once described those who shared his profession as "underpaid and overprivileged," and that's as good a definition as you'll ever get of the life of a golf writer. Imagine a job that allows you to play golf with Sam Snead, then spend hours listening to the Great Man weave a tapestry of the past fifty years from his unique perspective. Or one that lets you sit with Gene Sarazen at the Masters as he reminisces about his dear friends Bob Jones, Walter Hagen, and Francis Ouimet. Or one that pays you to go beer to beer with Lee Trevino as he describes his love for—and fascination with—the game that lifted him from the worst poverty to companionship with the world's movers and shakers.

In locker rooms, pressrooms, and grillrooms around the world I've heard hundreds, maybe thousands, of stories. Some were funny. Some were touching. To be sure, some of the stories in this book will be familiar to golfers, but like all good tales they often improve in the retelling: a new twist is added, a different spin is put on the ball. So much the better for everyone concerned.

Some of these stories may be apocryphal. No matter, really, for they have added richly to the lore, beauty, and joy of the game—and, I hope, to your enjoyment of this book.

"And Then Jack Said to Arnie..."

AMY ALCOTT

"People think there's a lot of pressure in golf. Heck, I'll tell you what pressure really is. It's working as a short-order cook. If I don't play good, I don't win. If I screw up in the kitchen, some guy doesn't eat. You've got to love it, right?"

Amy Alcott is one of the best competitors, finest shot-makers, and funniest people in the game. The fact that she won the 1980 U.S. Women's Open at Richland Country Club in Nashville in heat that was over one hundred degrees each day proves my first point. ABC's Bob Rosburg, the 1959 PGA champion and a man not given to pulling his punches, once said that Amy was "the only player on the women's tour who can play shots." You'll have to take my word on her sense of humor.

Unlike many golfers of her generation, Amy didn't come from a family that played golf. She discovered the game on her own, as she explains:

"Neither of my parents played, and we didn't belong to a private club. One day I was watching cartoons on television, and the old 'Shell's Wonderful World of Golf' came on. I was completely awed by the beauty of the golf course and the way the players could make the ball do anything they wanted. I was addicted to that show and the CBS Golf Classic. In fact, until I was sixteen I thought all the good men players were named either Labron, Kermit, or 'Pards,' because all I heard them say was 'Nice shot, Pards' or 'You're away, Pards.' Come to think of it, I always thought 'Pards' was kind of a stupid name anyway."

●

*I*n my third year on tour I came to Westchester County, just outside New York City, for the Golden Lights Tournament at Wykagyl C.C. For a long time I had heard about the nearby Westchester C.C. and the hotel there so I thought that would be a good place to stay, even if it was over my budget," recalls Amy Alcott. "I played with a big executive from Hebrew National foods in the pro-am and we had a great time. The next day a package of his company's food arrived at the hotel. There were two chickens, pastrami, corned beef, hot dogs, a roast turkey—the works. I could have fed 50 people a day for the entire week. My room didn't have a refrigerator, so I didn't have a clue as to what to do with the food. On the way to the course the next day I noticed a huge trophy case in the lobby with a lot of old trophies and some flowers. When I saw the flowers I realized the case was refrigerated, so I decided to store the food in the showcase. I had the chef at the clubhouse slice up the meats. I stopped at a local deli and got some cole slaw, potato salad, and other stuff, and then I invited people over for meals every night. Heck, I used to sneak down into the lobby in my bathhrobe for midnight snacks. A couple years ago I was talking to Hale Irwin about our favorite courses. He mentioned Westchester, and I told him that not only was it one of my favorite courses, but its lobby was one of my favorite places to eat."

*A*my's nine-shot victory in the 1980 Women's Open is generally considered to be one of the great wins on any tour. In the searing heat and humidity, she was the only player to break par.

In the final round she was paired with her longtime rival Hollis Stacy. As Amy, on the verge of exhaustion and dehydration, approached the last green, Hollis walked over and said, "Amy, whatever you do, don't fifteen-putt."

AUGUSTA NATIONAL GOLF CLUB

"Nothing funny ever happens at Augusta. Dogs don't bark and babies don't cry. They wouldn't dare."
—CBS Sports Producer/Director Frank Chirkinian

The Augusta National Golf Club in Augusta, Georgia, may be the best-known course in the world, since it is the site of the Masters Tournament each spring.

No matter how often you see the course on television, nothing can quite prepare you for the experience of seeing the place in person. The course is stunning in its scale and scope, and in the spring, when the thousands of flowers and shrubs are in bloom, the scene can take your breath away. When I arrived for my first Masters, I had the good fortune to run into Ken Bowden, a transplanted British journalist who works with Jack Nicklaus. He advised me to walk the course from beginning to end, taking time to savor the splendor of the scene. This year will be my tenth Masters, and every year I make a point of taking the same walk—and each time I'm more impressed than I was the year before.

But it's not just the sheer beauty of Augusta that leaves such an impression. There's the history and rich legacy left by men such as Bob Jones, Clifford Roberts, Dwight Eisenhower, and all the champions who have measured themselves in this most singular tournament—a Major that signals the unofficial start of the golf year and yet is not really the championship of anything. There's the respect shown to both amateurs and international players, the utter contempt for commercialism, and the enthusiasm of the galleries, among the most knowledgeable in golf.

Augusta is also one of the most exclusive clubs in the world. Membership is by invitation only, and for many years the club was run by its autocratic chairman, Clifford Roberts, a Wall Street financier who had total control over the place, including the comings and goings on the membership roster. If Roberts decided you were no longer going to be a member, you were history. No letter. No appeal. According to one story, the process went something like this:

A member called the club to arrange for a visit and a stay in one of the cabins. The switchboard connected him with Mr. Roberts, who informed him that he was no longer a member.

"For what reason, Cliff?" the astonished man asked.

"Nonpayment of your bill," said Roberts coldly.

"But I never received a bill," the member protested.

"Exactly," said Roberts, as he hung up the phone.

●

*O*ne of the most prominent members of Augusta National was President Dwight D. Eisenhower. But even the president of the United States, the former supreme commander of all the Allied forces in Europe in World War II, couldn't intimidate Clifford Roberts. A case in point was a tree on the 17th hole that Ike drove into with stunning regularity. He frequently protested the existence of the tree, requesting time after time that it be cut down. Roberts wouldn't hear of it, but he did acknowledge the president's efforts by naming it "Ike's Tree."

●

*U*nknown to many people is the role that Cypress Point Golf Club, a continent away from Augusta on the Pacific Ocean, played in the development of Augusta National.

Bob Jones traveled to Pebble Beach for the 1929 U.S. Amateur. There he was upset in the first round by twenty-one-year-old Johnny Goodman, who had traveled west from Omaha in a cattle car. Goodman would go on to win the 1933 and 1937 U.S. Opens, but in 1929 he was virtually unknown.

With time on his hands, Jones played several local courses and fell under Cypress Point's spell. At the same time, he met the course's designer, Dr. Alister Mackenzie, a Scottish-born architect of considerable merit. He was so taken by Mackenzie and his work that he inquired whether Mackenzie would be interested in building a course with him.

Clearly no one could turn down such an invitation, and when Jones and his friends found the perfect property in the old Berckman's Nursery, all the pieces finally came into place.

As another sidelight to the story, it's said that when Donald Ross, the preeminent architect of the day, learned that Jones had selected Mackenzie to design Augusta National, he devoted his considerable energies and talents to the design of Pinehurst No. 2, in order to build the supreme course of the day. Many believe he succeeded.

*O*ne of the reasons the Masters Tournament has become so special is the attention that is paid to every detail. The tournament has long been televised by CBS Sports under a series of one-year contracts that help ensure that the telecasts are done in a manner agreeable to club officials. One strictly held tenet is that there are limited commercial interruptions. One year Clifford Roberts decided he wanted this made clear to the audience and asked—ordered, actually—CBS to come up with an appropriate spokesman to make that announcement at the beginning of the broadcasts. A CBS executive suggested Ed Sullivan.

"Ed Sullivan!" roared Roberts. "If we wanted someone from show business we'd get Randolph Scott."

●

*T*he people who run the Masters place great emphasis on decorum. You can imagine their reaction when they learned that a bunch of college students had hired a stripper to streak the 16th green on the final day of the Masters.

"Cliff Roberts had heard that she was going to run out of the gallery as soon as she saw the red light of our camera go on," recalls Frank Chirkinian of CBS Sports. "The kids had her payment and bail money all set. I told Cliff not to worry, that we'd just disconnect the light and they'd never know when the camera was on. That didn't satisfy him. He told the security people that he wanted her arrested immediately, and he stressed that he personally wanted her entrance badge. She never did appear, and I've always wondered just where Cliff thought she was going to be wearing her badge in the first place."

*T*he Masters has always made a special effort to include the best amateur players in its field, a tradition spawned by Bob Jones's career as the greatest amateur golfer in history. Still, no matter how good an amateur might be, playing in the Masters is an unnerving experience. Consider the case of James Taylor, the 1989 United States Mid-Amateur champion, who was paired with Arnold Palmer in the 1990 Masters.

He hit his drive on the dogleg left, par-5 13th hole, but when he reached the landing area his ball was nowhere to be found. Since he hadn't hit a provisional, he had to suffer the humiliation of walking back to the tee, where the next group was waiting and watching.

"Take your time, Jim," said Peter Jacobsen. "We just love watching you swing."

●

*T*he 155-yard, par-3 12th hole at Augusta National is one of the best holes in the world. It's also one of the most terrifying. The shallow green is guarded in front by Rae's Creek and a bunker. There's another bunker behind the green, along with the usual assortment of flora and fauna, which looks beautiful until your ball sails merrily into it. But what really makes the 12th so damned hard is the wind, which gusts and swirls and makes club selection maddening. All in all, the 12th has killed more guys than Audie Murphy. Here are some examples:

Bob Rosburg, the 1959 PGA champion, came to the 12th one year and went with a 4-iron. Rossie swung. The wind died. The ball easily cleared the water . . . and the front bunker . . . and the green, the back bunker, the gorgeous flowering whatevers, and a fence, coming to rest on the 9th hole at the adjoining Augusta Country Club (or as Hord Hardin, Augusta National's chairman, calls it, "the club where they hold the dances.")

It's a testimonial to the Masters' prestige that Rossie didn't elect to walk in and head for the nearest racetrack, as he was wont to do. Instead, he re-teed, hit another 4-iron to fifteen feet, and made the putt for a truly world-class five.

•

Curtis Strange came to the hole in the 1988 Masters hot on the heels of four-putting the 9th hole. "Hot" is the operative word here, for few players loathe things like four-putting as much as Curtis. With the pin cut to the right-hand side of the green (a pin position Jack Nicklaus says he never, ever, shoots at), Curtis aimed at the center of the green and, as he says, "pushed it perfectly." The ball dropped in for an ace, only the third on that hole in Masters history.

When he reached the green, Curtis took the ball from the cup and tossed it into Rae's Creek. This thrilled the fans but upset some writers who thought he should have given it to Golf House or Hord, or whatever. One suggested he should have saved it for his grandchildren. "I hope I have something better to leave my grandchildren than a golf ball," Curtis replied, logically enough.

•

In 1980 Tom Weiskopf came to the 12th hole in the first round. The pin was cut in the easiest position—front left—and, for a change, there was no wind to complicate matters. Weiskopf, a player who lived for the Masters, took an 8-iron, hit the green, then watched in dismay as the ball checked back off the green and rolled into the

9

water. He took a drop, hit again, and watched as the ball tumbled into the creek. By the time the smoke had cleared he had made a 13, the highest score on either a par 3 or par 4 in Masters history.

As she watched her husband's hopes wash down Rae's Creek, Jeanne Weiskopf began to cry. A friend, Tom Culver, put his arms around her and asked, "Jeanne, you don't suppose he's using new balls, do you?"

•

Finally, in 1963 Tony Lema came to the 12th after missing a short putt on 10 and three-putting 11. His tee shot stopped eight feet from the hole, but he missed the putt, which prompted a glittering display of verbal pyrotechnics. Embarrassed by his outburst, he turned to his playing companion, Chen Ching-po from Nationalist China, and apologized.

"It's all right," said Chen. "If I only knew those words I would use them myself."

MILLER BARBER

I've always thought that Miller Barber is a wonderful testimonial to how mysterious the golf swing truly is. At a time when computer scientists and cosmic thinkers of every sort are employing the highest of high-tech stuff to create ideal swing models, and players at every level have highly paid professionals on retainer to fine-tune their moves, here's Miller Barber with a swing that looks like an accident waiting to happen, but he is still one of the best ball-strikers in the business.

For much of his career, Miller has been known as "Mr. X." If you think that's because of his sunglasses, think again.

"I won the Seattle Open in 1961," remembers Dave Marr, winner of the 1965 PGA Championship and ABC commentator. "Just to show you how things were in those days, my check was $4,000, but Miller got $10,000 for making a hole-in-one. Now this was before Miller had really established himself on tour, so as we were planning to leave for the Del Webb tournament in Bakersfield on Sunday, Jim Ferree asked Miller to drive his car down so he could fly. That was fine with Miller, who was single at the time. We got to Bakersfield, but Miller never showed up. He finally surfaced a week or so later at another tournament. He never would tell us where he was. Still won't to this day. All we know for sure is he had Jimmy's car, $10,000, and a case of Canadian Club that Jimmy had brought down from Canada for his dad. When Miller caught up with us, there was only one bottle left. That's how Miller got the name 'the Mysterious Mr. X.'"

AL BESSELINK

*A*l Besselink joined the tour in 1950 and won a handful of tournaments by the early 60s. "Bessie was what you'd call an original," says Dave Marr. "He was one of the nicest guys in the world, but it seemed like he was always broke. You wanted to help him out, but if you loaned him money you could color it gone. He was the kind of guy that would be more than happy to loan you every cent he had. The problem was, he never had any.

"Anyway, Bessie's at a track in Miami, and he's completely tapped out. He's supposed to go down to South America and play, but he doesn't have the bus fare to get across town. As would happen with Bessie, he kicked over a ticket for a winner—I mean, what are the odds of that?—and it paid enough for him to get south and make some money. He went down there and did very well for himself, but of course it never made the papers up here. He got to the Desert Inn in Las Vegas for the first Tournament of Champions and found himself the long shot. But Bessie knew he was playing good, even if no one else did, so he bet a ton on himself. He not only won the bet, but he won ten thousand silver dollars, which was just a huge purse. Typical of Bessie, though, he gave a whole bunch of his winnings to the Damon Runyon Cancer Fund and never made a big deal about it."

HOMERO BLANCAS

*H*omero Blancas is the son of a greenskeeper at the River Oaks Country Club in Houston. He won his share of tournaments on tour in the late 60s and early 70s, but his greatest acclaim came from his play at the University of Houston, where he was a legend—in no small part because of his performance one year at the Premier Invitational, a college tournament in Longview, Texas.

Fred Marti was Blancas's teammate at Houston and a fine golfer in his own right. He had a practice of calling his father during a tournament to let him know how he was doing. He called after the first round to tell his dad that he had shot a 61 on the par-70 course.

"Great playing, Fred," said his father. "How many shots does that put you in the lead?"

"I'm a shot back, Dad," Marti said. "One of the other Houston guys shot a 60. His name's Homero Blancas, and he's a hell of a player."

"Don't worry about it, son," said his father. "One hot round doesn't mean a thing. He's bound to blow up. Just play your own game."

The next day Marti called in with the final results. He had shot another 61.

"Good Lord Almighty, Fred," his father said. "I'm proud

13

of you, son. That's just great playing. I hope that Blancas boy didn't take it too hard."

"Not really, Dad," Marti said.

"Did he stay close?" Mr. Marti asked.

"Sort of," his son answered. "We were within seven shots."

"That's a fine showing, Fred. He has nothing to be ashamed of," said Mr. Marti.

"I guess not, Dad," said Fred. "He shot a 55."

TOMMY BOLT

"Tommy Bolt's putter has more air time than Lindbergh."

—Jimmy Demaret

A sk players or writers to name the greatest golfers in history and you get pretty much the same list—Nicklaus, Snead, Nelson, Hogan, Jones, and so on. But when you ask who had the best swing or was the best shotmaker, you add at least one new name to the list: Tommy Bolt. He was born in Haworth, Oklahoma, a place he described as "so damn deep in the woods they had to pipe light in."

Sadly, Bolt never gets the credit he deserves for his skills. Lee Trevino ranks him among the five best players he ever saw. Tom Weiskopf, another artist with his clubs, is still in awe of Bolt's ability to fashion shots. But most people think of him as "Terrible-Tempered Tommy Bolt" or "Thunder Bolt" for his—how should we say this?—willingness to wear his emotions on his sleeve. The truth is, Tommy has always been good copy and did a lot to popularize the game in the 1950s and 1960s. That he isn't in the World Golf Hall of Fame is a shame.

*L*eading the 1958 U.S. Open, he stormed into the pressroom one day looking for Tom Lobaugh, who was covering the championship for a local paper, the *Tulsa World*. Summoning all his righteous indignation, he berated Lobaugh for reporting that Bolt was forty-nine instead of thirty-nine.

"Sorry, Tommy, it was a typo," said Lobaugh.

"Typo, my ass," said Bolt. "It was a perfect four and a perfect nine."

●

*B*olt had a well-deserved reputation for throwing clubs, although he always protested that if he threw and broke as many clubs as people claimed, "the entire damned equipment business in this country would have spent their time making clubs for Old Tom, don't ya see?"

Anyway, the story goes that in one tournament Tommy came into the final hole facing a 120-yard shot to the green. His caddie handed him a 3-iron.

"What the hell is this, son?" he fumed, "I can hit this club almost 200 yards."

"I know, sir," the caddie said. "But it's the only iron you have left. You broke all the rest."

By the way, Tommy always takes credit for giving Arnold Palmer a valuable lesson when Palmer first came out on tour.

"I had to take the boy aside and teach him how to throw a club," recalls Tommy. "He was so innocent he'd toss them backwards. I had to explain that you'd get worn out walking back to pick them up. You have to throw them in front of you if you're going to be a professional."

*T*ommy Bolt never believed he got as many good breaks as bad. One day, after missing yet another short putt, he tossed down his putter and glared at the heavens.

"So it's me again, huh, Lord?" he grimaced. "Why don't you just come down here and we'll play? And bring that kid of yours. I'll play your best ball."

●

*O*ne day, while playing in a pro-am, Bolt drew a partner who was not a very good player in the first place. Naturally, playing with Tommy made him nervous, which only made things worse. The man shanked every shot on the first hole. Embarrassed, he turned to Bolt and apologized, asking if Tommy had any advice for him.

"Yes," said Tommy. "Just aim left and allow for it."

●

*I*t's not that Tommy didn't try to help his amateur partners. One story holds that Tommy once tried to fix a pro-am partner's poor grip.

"With a grip like that, I don't expect you hit it very straight," Tommy said.

"Well, yes, Tommy," he replied. "As a matter of fact, I'm very straight with every club."

"Then you can't possibly hit it very far," said Tommy.

"Actually, I'm one of the longest players at my club," came the reply.

"Well, you must play a lot then, son," said Tommy, becoming increasingly frustrated that his attempts at instruction were getting so complicated.

"No, Tom," said the amateur. "I hardly play at all."

"Well, that explains it," said Tommy, walking away. "The more you play with a grip like that, the worse you're going to get."

●

As one might expect, Tommy Bolt didn't have much use for authority and, indeed, delighted in flaunting it.

Playing a practice round for a tournament just after his 1958 Open win, he ignored the rule requiring players to use just one ball during their round. He hit three balls into a green before being interrupted by a tournament official.

"Tommy, you know the one-ball rule is in effect," said the official. "I'm going to have to fine you $25 each for those two extra balls."

As the gallery looked on, Bolt reached into his pocket and pulled out a $100 bill.

"Here, son," he said. "Keep the change. I'm hitting two more."

●

Tommy was playing in Los Angeles one year, and prior to his round he told his caddie, Snake, not to say one word to him. Coming down the final stretch of holes, Tommy hit a drive that wound up behind a tree.

"What do you think about a 5-iron here?" he asked Snake, who, following orders, didn't reply.

Bolt fashioned a beautiful recovery, turned proudly to Snake, and said, "Well now, what the hell do you think of that?"

"That wasn't your ball, Mr. Bolt," he said, picking up the bag and heading down the fairway.

*W*hen Tom Weiskopf came out on tour, Tommy took him under his wing. Once, when playing in Ohio, Weiskopf arranged for a friend from Ohio State, Ed Sneed, to join them for a round.

When they reached a par 3, Sneed hit a draw that landed on the green, bounced once, and ran into the rough.

"My, my, Edgar, that was a fine shot you played there," Tommy said, as he strolled off the green. "Those old right-to-lefts will run on you, won't they, Ed?"

●

*I*n an era when most pros favored what Tommy called "those Ben Hogan blues and grays, " Bolt stood out as a truly wonderful dresser. In fact, nothing infuriated him more than hearing about Doug Sanders's sense of style.

"The man looks like a jukebox with feet," he once said. "In fact, even his feet look like jukeboxes."

●

*I*n 1958 Tommy won the U.S. Open, a championship he described as "a Ben Hogan-type tournament." That win would be the high point of his career. You could make the case that the low point came two years later when the Open came to Cherry Hills Country Club in Denver.

Nearing the close of a particularly frustrating round, Bolt came to the 18th hole and promptly snap-hooked two drives into a pond. With that, he strode to the front of the tee, studied the offending driver, and launched it into the pond, to the considerable amazement of the gallery.

In the crowd was a young boy who dived into the pond

and surfaced with Bolt's driver. Tommy approached the boy, money clip in hand, anxious to show his appreciation and check the club for damage. He never got the chance. The kid took off like a broken-field runner, raced through the gallery, and clambered over a fence, the roar of the crowd echoing in his ears.

To this day Tommy insists he didn't mean to throw the club into the water.

"It was just a hot day, and those worn grips got a little slick on Old Tom," he recalls. "Hell, I was just taking a practice swing for myself, and the next thing I knew that little beauty was sailing out over the water. It was a shame—I really liked that club too."

HARRY BRADSHAW

*I*reland's Harry Bradshaw had perhaps the most divine, if unique, training for the game of golf.

When Bradshaw was an adolescent, an elderly local priest, Father Gleason, saw that he had a talent for golf. Each evening they would go to a hole at Delgany with clubs, balls, a folding chair, and the Scriptures. Once there, Father Gleason would select a spot a hundred or so yards from the hole.

"Harry, you shall practice your approach shots, and we will not leave this place until you have holed one," said the priest, who would then ease back in his chair and turn his attention to the missal, occasionally pausing to read the boy a particularly enlightening or encouraging passage.

As a result of his training, Bradshaw developed not only a certain serenity for this most maddening of games but also an astonishingly skillful short game.

In the course of his career, he teamed with fellow countryman Christy O'Connor to win the 1958 World Cup against the best golfers in the world. In 1971 he was pitted against Billy Casper in a head-to-head match at Portmarnock. Casper, easily one of the best players in the game at that time, drew 7-1 odds from Dublin's bookies.

"I can understand the boys' thinking," Bradshaw said. "Casper would beat me anyplace else on earth, and easily enough, but at Portmarnock? If I were a betting man I might wager a pound or two on myself."

That was enough for the locals, who flooded the bookies with bets on the hometown boy—bets that paid off handsomely when Bradshaw neatly handled Casper.

•

*P*erhaps the best-known Harry Bradshaw story concerned his run-in with a broken bottle at the 1949 British Open at Royal St. George's. Bradshaw led after an opening-round 68. In the second round, his drive on the 14th hole sailed into the right rough, coming to rest in the bottom of a broken beer bottle. Bradshaw suspected he might be allowed relief, but since the clubhouse was so far away and he couldn't bear the thought of holding up play, he elected to play the ball from the bottle. Besides, taking advantage of the rules in such a way conflicted with his deeply held views of the game.

Taking a wedge, Bradshaw closed his eyes and smashed away at the ball, sending it and the shattered glass a mere twenty-five yards. The resulting six set the stage for a 77, which left him tied with South Africa's Bobby Locke. The men matched cards for the next two rounds before meeting in a 36-hole playoff, which Locke won by 12 strokes.

Some years later Bradshaw was asked if he ever regretted not seeking a ruling.

"Never for a single second," he replied. "True, if I had sent for a ruling I might have won the championship, but it would not have been right. Locke was by far the better player and deserved to win."

CADDIES

"Finally Hoyt appealed to me. I looked at ten-year-old Eddie, his eyes filled, and I think he was fearful that I would turn him down. In any event, he seemed so sincere I did not have the heart to take the clubs away from him, and my final gesture was to tell Steve that Eddie was going to caddie for me."

—Francis Ouimet, recounting his decision to keep Eddie Lowery as his caddie for the playoff in the 1913 U.S. Open, which he won

*P*eople say there's no good news anymore, but here's a sliver of hope: caddies are making a comeback. More and more are showing up at courses around the country hoping to earn a few bucks and learn about the game. And golfers are getting increasingly fed up with being forced to ride in carts.

Golf is a better game with a caddie. Good caddies share your highs and commiserate with your lows. They can even help your game . . . or at least try. Joe Rice, a favorite caddie of mine from home, is always threatening to "drop this bag and walk in" if he sees one more fast swing from me. He hasn't done it yet. And I'm afraid he's not likely to run out of opportunities any time soon.

For a writer, caddies are a great source of stories because they're just so damned human. Besides, when was the last time you heard a good story about an E-Z Go?

24

A group of wealthy Arab businessmen wearing tradi-
tional headdresses arrived at the Old Course at St.
Andrews for a round of golf. At the completion of his
round, one handed his caddie, an elderly Scotsman, a
generous tip.

"Thanks very much, your excellency," said the caddie.
"And I hope your head feels better."

●

T he greenside bunker on the 17th hole at the Old
Course is one of the most feared and noteworthy
hazards in the game. Years ago an American tourist came
to the 17th at the close of what had already been a long
and frustrating round. That he managed to wind up in the
bunker came as no surprise to his caddie. Neither did the
fact that he couldn't manage to extricate himself.

"What should I take?" he asked the caddie.
"How about the 7:30 train to Dundee?" came the reply.

●

Y ears ago, the caddies on the tours weren't nearly as
professional as they are today. In fact, often they were
just local kids without much experience or knowledge of
the game. Julius Boros ran into just one such kid.

After hitting his approach to the first hole, Boros
pointed to his divot and told the caddie to pick it up. As
the round progressed, the boy fell farther and farther
behind. Boros, thinking the caddie had become ill, asked
him if he was feeling all right.

"Yes, sir, but I was just wondering what you want me
to do with all these?" he said, opening the side pocket of
Boros's bag, which was filled with divots.

*H*erman Mitchell is best known as Lee Trevino's caddie, but he also caddied for Miller Barber for many years. Once as they stood on the tee on a dogleg, he asked Herman what was behind the bunker guarding the corner.

"Double bogey, double bogey, and double bogey," said Herman.

Since teaming with Lee Trevino, Herman has been fighting an on-again, off-again battle with his weight. At one point, Trevino talked him into eating less junk food and more fruit, only to find out he was eating huge quantities of the stuff at every sitting.

"Damn, Herman, just 'cause you're eating fruit doesn't mean you can eat all you want. There's an 800 pound gorilla over in the Dallas Zoo, and all he eats is fruit too."

●

*G*ene Sarazen played himself into contention in the 1928 British Open at Royal St. George's but ignored the advice of his caddie, Skip Daniels. The resulting errors cost him the championship, and he finished second to his old friend and rival Walter Hagen.

Sarazen was bitterly disappointed, but Daniels pledged to him, "Before I die, I'm going to win the Open Championship for you."

Four years later, at Prince's, Sarazen won with Daniels at his side. A few months later Daniels, who had been sick throughout the championship, died quietly, his promises having been kept.

*B*obby Cruickshank came to Muirfield for the 1929 British Open and drew a seventy-year-old caddie, Willie Black. After hitting a good drive on the first hole of a practice round, Cruickshank asked Willie for a 2-iron.

"See here, sir," said Willie. "I'll give you the club, you just play the bloody shot."

On another occasion, Cruickshank was set to play his approach with a fairway wood. Suddenly, at the top of his backswing, Willie shouted, "Stop! We've changed our mind. We'll play the shot with an iron."

●

*F*rank Stranahan was a two-time winner of the British Amateur, but that did not particularly endear the American to the caddies when he traveled to Muirfield for the 1954 British Amateur. He clashed repeatedly with his caddies, firing several of them.

Finally the caddies got their revenge when Stranahan faced an approach to a green hidden behind a ridge. He sent his caddie ahead to give him a line for his shot, the caddie paced along the ridge, looking first to Stranahan and then back toward the green. Finally he signaled Stranahan to play away. Stranahan's shot whistled over the caddie's head, but when he reached the crest of the hill he saw that his ball was nestled deep in a thick stand of gorse.

"Now, Mr. Stranahan, sir, if you think you know so damn much about it, let's see you get yourself out of there," said the caddie, laying the bag at Stranahan's feet and striding off for the clubhouse.

*D*ave Marr was playing a practice round in a British Open and stood over his approach to a par 4. He asked his caddie what club he should hit.

"A 6-iron, sir," his caddie said.

"A hard six or an easy six?" Marr asked.

"Just the true measure of the club," came the reply.

●

*A*n American visiting Scotland for the first time was gushing to his caddie about the beauties of the game. When he finished his praise of the gorse and the heather and the challenge of it all, he concluded by saying that what he liked best about the game was that it was so "friendly."

" 'Twasn't meant to be," growled the caddie.

●

*T*he Scots have a much simpler, almost reverential, approach to the game, unlike Americans who complicate the game by mimicking the things they see the pros do on television—stuff that doesn't help their games but only manages to slow down play.

Take the story of the American who showed up at St. Andrews with his huge, heavy bag, high-tech clubs, and most fashionable clothes.

Upon reaching his opening drive, he reached down, clipped a bit of grass, and tossed it into the air to check the wind.

"What do you think?" he asked his caddie.

The caddie responded by mimicking the player and tossing the few blades of grass into the air.

"I think the wind's come up, governor," said the caddie. "You'd best take out your sweater."

A foursome was playing at The Homestead, the elegant old resort tucked high in the mountains of western Virginia.

When they came to a par 3, they saw a pair of wild turkeys on the green. Surprised, they asked their caddie if it was unusual to see turkeys on the greens.

"Well, them birds have a keen sense of danger, but I don't reckon there's much chance of them getting hit by anyone in this group," he said.

●

*T*ip Anderson has achieved a certain renown as Arnold Palmer's longtime caddie in the British Open. It's not uncommon for players to ask Tip what Palmer would hit in a certain situation and then try the shot themselves.

In one case, a friend of Palmer's came to St. Andrews and drew Tip as a caddie. When they came to the 4th hole, he faced a long, difficult approach to green. He asked for the same club Palmer had hit from that spot, but his ball came up forty yards short of the green.

"I can't believe Arnold got there with this club," he said to Tip.

"Oh, he didn't, sir," Tip said. "He came up well short, too."

●

*M*ad Mac was a Scottish caddie whose wardrobe consisted almost exclusively of a long, woolen overcoat which he wore regardless of the weather. He also favored a pair of binoculars without lenses, through which he'd study the line of a putt before announcing that it was "slightly straight."

29

*F*rancis Ouimet was playing in the British Open one year and had a typically strong-willed caddie. Facing a different approach shot, he wanted to hit a mashie niblick, while his caddie insisted the shot called for a jigger. They went back and forth until Ouimet finally decided to hit the mashie niblick, which he holed.

"Aye, ye would have done better with the jigger," said the caddie as he marched off toward the next tee in a huff.

•

*R*aymond Floyd was playing in the 1981 British Open at Royal St. George's. Facing a blind drive over a string of mounds, he asked his caddie for the line.

"Just hit it over the third hump," said the caddie confidently.

Floyd blistered a drive, but when he reached his ball he found it resting in grass up to his knees. He glared at his caddie.

"Wrong hump, governor," shrugged his caddie.

WILLIAM C. CAMPBELL

*B*ill Campbell is often held up as the ideal amateur—
a man of impeccable rectitude who loves the game for
its own sake.

A former president of the United States Golf Association, captain of the Royal and Ancient Golf Club of St.
Andrews, a U.S. Amateur champion, and member and
captain of America's Walker Cup teams—all that just for
starters—he is one of the last of what is, sadly, a dying
breed—the true, lifelong amateur.

Once, when Jack Nicklaus and Frank Hannigan, then
senior executive director of the USGA, were having a
discussion concerning the strict rules of amateur status,
Nicklaus challenged Hannigan to name one prominent
amateur who didn't receive free equipment.

"Bill Campbell," replied Hannigan without hesitation.

"I'll give you Bill Campbell," Nicklaus answered.
"Name one other."

●

*B*ill Campbell knows the value of a buck. In fact,
friends say he's the only player who ever showed up at
the first tee at the Masters and wondered where the
ballwasher was.

JoANNE CARNER

"Billy Martin taught me a lot about being a good competitor. In fact, the only thing he never tried to teach me was how to knock a guy out in a bar."
     —JoAnne Carner, on her friendship
     with the late Billy Martin

I can't think of anyone who has brought more joy to the pursuit of golf at the highest level than JoAnne Carner. Only Jack Nicklaus and Bob Jones have won more USGA National Championships than Carner, and she accomplished all this while maintaining the ability to laugh at both herself and this most maddening of games.

Once, after watching her play the final round of an LPGA Championship, I interviewed her for a story. In the course of the interview I mentioned that she seemed unusually serious, almost grim, on television.

"I was trying to smile, but I was choking so badly my lips stuck to my teeth," she laughed.

I was playing in the Women's Open at Baltimore Country Club at Five Farms and faced a blind approach shot. I sent my caddie ahead and told him to stand on the hill and give me a line to the green. Once I saw him stop on the hill, I pulled a club from the bag and played my shot, pulling it well to the left. God, was I hot! As I came up over the hill the gallery was cheering like crazy. I looked down to the green, and my ball was next to the cup. I turned to my caddie and asked him what line he thought he was giving me."

" 'I was trying to show you where *not* to hit it, but you played so fast I didn't have time to yell down and tell you,' he said.

"That's the thing about golf. Sometimes it's better to be lucky than good."

●

B ack in the late 1970s and early 1980s, Ray Volpe, then the commissioner of the LPGA, decided something needed to be done to give his players a, well, sexier image. The result was a series of photos that showed LPGA players in a variety of somewhat revealing poses. Most notable was a photo of Jan Stephenson showing a little—okay, actually a lot of—thigh.

Predictably, some of the players found the whole business sexist and offensive, and the ensuing controversy generated miles of publicity—which is just what Volpe had in mind. One player who liked the whole idea was JoAnne Carner.

"I don't understand what the excitement's about," she said. "I wish they'd ask me to pose. In fact, I think they needed a little cellulite. They should include a 'Miss Piggy' of the LPGA Tour."

DICK CHAPMAN

*D*ick Chapman was an outstanding amateur in the 1940s and 1950s, winning both the U.S. and British Amateurs and playing with distinction on a number of American Walker Cup teams.

Chapman won the 1940 U.S. Amateur at Winged Foot. That he won wasn't really a surprise, but the circumstances surrounding his win were eerie, to say the least.

In 1929, as an eighteen-year-old, Chapman had traveled the few miles from his home in Greenwich, Connecticut, to Winged Foot with his father to watch Bob Jones win a U.S. Open playoff with Al Espinosa.

Chapman and his father happened to be standing on the right side of the 9th fairway, in the area where Jones hit his drive. After watching Jones play his second shot, Chapman turned to his father and said, "I'd love to someday be in Jones's shoes, winning a national championship."

"Someday you will, Dick," said his father.

Eleven years later, Chapman came to the same hole, ten up with ten to play in the finals of the amateur championship. His drive came to rest in virtually the same spot as Jones's had years before.

Just before hitting his approach to what turned out to be the final green, Chapman swore he heard his father say, "Dick, here it is, son. You said you wanted it. This is it."

FRANK CHIRKINIAN

"Cut your talking in half. You're not saying anything interesting anyway."
    —Frank Chirkinian to his commentators, in Dan Jenkins's *The Dogged Victims of Inexorable Fate*

*W*hen I first came to *Golf Digest* in the late 1970s, I was assigned a two-part series on what was wrong with television coverage of golf. Owing to my keen reportorial instincts, I decided to begin with the guy who had been producing and directing golf on television the longest—Frank Chirkinian of CBS Sports.

He invited me to join him and his wife, Mary Jane, for dinner in Los Angeles. When I arrived, he introduced me by saying: "Mary Jane, this is the smart son of a bitch that's going to tell us what I've been doing wrong all these years."

Wonderful. Thirteen years later, I still don't know what's wrong with golf on television, except that everybody with a typewriter and a television seems to be an expert on it—and it's not nearly as much fun as it used to be.

One year, while Chirkinian was directing a segment of the old CBS Golf Classic, Bruce Crampton made a hole-in-one. Now Crampton can be a fairly icy character, and he turned to the announcer and asked what he got for making the ace.

"Tell Bruce he gets the honor on the next tee and to speed things up. We don't have all day," came Chirkinian's reply.

•

One time Kenny [Venturi] and I met Ben Hogan for lunch at Shady Oaks. Following lunch we were down in the locker room, and Ben decided to demonstrate one of his secrets for getting power, which had something to do with his forearms. When I asked him about it he said, 'See, I knew I shouldn't have told you two, now you'll tell everyone.' "

" 'I won't tell anyone, Ben,' " promised Kenny.

" 'But he will,' " Ben said, pointing at me."

" 'Yeah, but who's gonna believe *him*?' Kenny asked."

•

I've been lucky to have a lot of good announcers to work with over the years, but they didn't always start out with so much promise. The first year Frank Glieber and Pat Summerall did the Masters, I told them to go up to the putting green and familiarize themselves with the players. When they got there, they saw a bag with 'Dunlop' written on the side.

" 'Let's go find Kenny [Venturi] and see what he knows about this Dunlop guy,' " Pat said to Frank."

37

WINSTON CHURCHILL

"Golf is a game whose aim is to hit a very small ball into a very small hole, with weapons singularly ill designed for the purpose."

THE CONCORD HOTEL

Golf has long been used as a way to attract guests to hotels and resorts, and that's particularly true in areas where there is fierce competition for customers. One such area is the Catskills, just north of New York City.

When Arthur Winarick, a barber who made a fortune selling hair-care products, built the Concord hotel, he was determined not to be outdone by his competition. When he learned that his archrival, Grossinger's Hotel, was building a new 18-hole course, he scoffed: "Eighteen holes! That's nothing. We'll build a 50-hole golf course and show them!"

In the end he settled for two 18s and a 9.

38

BEN CRENSHAW

"Golf is the hardest game in the world. There's no way you can ever get it. Just when you think you do, the game jumps up and puts you into your place."

—Ben Crenshaw

*T*he next person I meet who doesn't like Ben Crenshaw will also be the first person I've met who doesn't like him. When Ben came out of the University of Texas he was billed as the next Jack Nicklaus. Of course, there never will be another Nicklaus, but Crenshaw has enjoyed a successful career capped by his emotional win in the 1984 Masters. His reputation as one of the finest putters in history belies a beautiful and powerful swing and an almost eerie touch. But he is more than a great player. He's a student of the game—its art, literature, and history. A purist, he's the first to admit that his work in course architecture is a throwback to an earlier age.

Throughout his somewhat up-and-down career, people have argued that Ben Crenshaw may just be too nice for his own good. They may be right, for Lord Acton's axiom holds that "no great man was ever a nice man." But if a person is going to be damned for something, being too damned nice isn't all bad.

*B*en Crenshaw was a fine all-around athlete as a boy growing up in Austin, Texas. He was particularly good in baseball, but at age nine his father suggested he take a shot at golf. As luck would have it, the professional at Austin Country Club was Harvey Penick, one of the most respected teachers in golf.

Mr. Penick took Ben out on a hole, put a ball down, and told Ben to hit it, which he did, putting it safely on the green.

"That's fine, Ben," he said. "Now let's go on up and see you knock it in the hole."

"Golly, Mr. Penick," Crenshaw said. "Why didn't you tell me that in the first place?"

With that, he dropped another ball and hit it into the cup.

●

*T*here may not be a player on tour with Ben Crenshaw's love of golf history. His knowledge has helped him at least once—in the 1984 Masters.

In the final round of the 1984 Masters, he hit a fine drive on the par 5 13th, a hole that tempts you to try to reach the green in two but punishes an errant play with water, sand, and psychological hazards of every sort.

As he pondered his second shot, he looked over to the right, to the gallery. There he saw Billy Joe Patton. In 1954 Patton, an outstanding amateur, led Sam Snead and Ben Hogan by a shot coming to this hole in the final round. After a good drive, Patton attacked the green with a 4-wood, only to watch in horror as a swirling gust of wind knocked his ball into the water fronting the green. His resulting double-bogey 7 cost him the tournament, as he finished a stroke behind Hogan and Snead. Snead went on to win the playoff the following day.

Back to 1984. Crenshaw took Patton's appearance as a sign, a warning to lay up and settle for a safe par, which he did. Crenshaw went on to win the tournament by two strokes over Tom Watson.

Good fortune? Perhaps, but Patton insists he was far away from 13 when Crenshaw played the hole.

●

*B*en was always such a likable youngster that the boys on the University of Texas golf team enjoyed having him around," recalls Harvey Penick. "One day he came out to watch the team practice. We were standing on the tee when these two real long hitters from West Texas came along and teed off. They just crushed the ball about three hundred yards each. I could see that Ben was in awe of those boys, so I leaned over to him and, in a soft voice, said, 'Ben, always remember—the woods are full of long hitters.' "

●

*L*ike most outstanding shotmakers, Crenshaw does have a stubborn side. Now and again, he'll try to hit a shot regardless of the consequences. That happened one year at the Heritage Classic, on the difficult, 153-yard, par 3 14th hole at Harbour Town Golf Links.

Crenshaw stood on the tee and hit three balls into the water fronting the green. He eventually took a nine but remained philosophical about the experience.

"Gosh darn it, I just knew I had the right club if I'd only hit the shot I wanted," he said. "Besides, after 14 I settled down and bogeyed the next three holes."

BING CROSBY

"Two of my favorite celebrities are comedian Bing Crosby and singer Bob Hope. Or is it the other way around? I always forget which one thinks he's funny and which one thinks he can sing."

—Jimmy Demaret

*B*ing Crosby may have been the best of the so-called celebrity golfers America has ever produced. He was accomplished enough to play in the U.S. and British Amateur championships. Playing in the 1940 U.S. Amateur at Winged Foot, he attracted such huge galleries that he required a police escort on the course. His son Nathaniel, won the U.S. Amateur in 1981, wearing his father's competitor's medal for good luck. At that time, ABC's Dave Marr was asked whether he thought Bing was up in heaven working a rosary. "I don't know about that, but he's probably humming a few bars of 'Straight Down the Middle.' "

●

*C*rosby played most of his golf at the Lakeside Golf Club in Los Angeles. One day he came out on the short end of a close match with a guy named John "Mysterious" Montague. Crosby hated to lose, and he hated to pay off his bets even more. After the match he was complaining, and Montague, who was known to hustle a bet now and then, said "Bing, I can handle you with a shovel, a bat, and a rake."

Crosby, a single-figure handicap, couldn't believe his ears and decided to play Montague for the money he had lost earlier, double or nothing.

Crosby hit the green in two, leaving himself a thirty-foot approach putt. Montague hit the ball with the bat twice, leaving his second shot in a greenside bunker. After Crosby hit his first putt three feet from the hole, Montague gave him the short putt and proceeded to scrape the ball out of the bunker with the shovel. Then, using the rake like a pool cue, he calmly ran in his putt.

Crosby then did the only logical thing he could think of. He shook his head and headed back to the clubhouse for a stiff drink.

●

One time Bob Hope and Jimmy Demaret beat Bing Crosby and Byron Nelson for $20. Crosby told Hope he'd pay him later, but the money was a long time coming.

Finally, one day Hope happened to stroll into the pro shop at Lakeside just as Crosby was getting change for a $100 bill. Hope, seeing his chance, swooped in, took his $20, and raced out the door, with Crosby hot on his heels. The footrace emptied the grillroom. Never in the annals of celebrity golf had one worked so hard to get his $20—or another man worked so hard to keep it.

*O*n a vacation to Scotland, Crosby and Phil Harris happened to drive past a scotch distillery following a late round of golf.

"Look, Phil, they're making the stuff faster than you can drink it," Crosby said.

"Yeah, but I've got them working nights," Harris replied.

BERNARD DARWIN

"Golf is not a funeral, although both can be very sad affairs."

—Bernard Darwin

*B*ernard Darwin was the longtime golf columnist of the *Times* of London. A semifinalist in the British Amateur, he filled in as a last-minute replacement in the 1922 Walker Cup at the National Golf Links, winning his singles match. Darwin, unlike virtually every other writer, never saw much point in quoting players about their rounds. "My readers," he once noted, "are not interested in what the pros say. They want to know what I thought." Indeed, Harry Vardon once said, "I never know how well I have played until I read Mr. Darwin's verdict in the next day's *Times*." He covered every great player from Vardon to Nicklaus before his death in 1961.

●

I was at Muirfield for the 1959 Walker Cup matches, and as my teammate Ward Wettlaufer and I were leaving the clubhouse we ran into Bernard Darwin," recalls Jack Nicklaus. "Ward was wearing a striped shirt that, while very tame by today's standards, was pretty daring for those days. Mr. Darwin, who was in his eighties at that point, looked at Ward's shirt and said, 'Tell me, dear boy, are those your old school colors or are they of your own unfortunate choosing?' "

JIMMY DEMARET

"If Jimmy Demaret had won the money he would have been eight to five to leave it in a bar or blow it on a handmade pair of orange and purple saddle oxfords."
—Dan Jenkins, *The Dogged Victims of Inexorable Fate*

Jimmy Demaret practiced less and had more fun than any other truly great player. He won three Masters, which Sam Snead always claimed was remarkable because "not only did Jimmy never practice, I don't think he ever slept."

Gardner Dickinson remembers his first trip to the Masters as a college student. "I went to the old Bon Air hotel, where all the players stayed," said Dickinson. "It was Saturday night, and there was Jimmy up on the stage, singing with the band and having one hell of a time for himself. He closed the place down about two in the morning. I saw him several hours later heading to the practice green just before his round. He looked like hell. He dropped a couple balls on the green, bent over to hit a putt, and went racing for the bushes, where he threw up. I said to myself, there's no damned way he's going to even play, much less win, but win is just what he did."

*O*ne year Jimmy Demaret was working as a commentator for a telecast of the Bing Crosby National Pro-Am from Pebble Beach. Arnold Palmer hit his drive on the par 3 17th over the green and down the cliff onto the beach.

As millions looked on, Palmer seemed at a loss to decide what to do next. Demaret was asked to explain the options offered by the unplayable lie rule.

"He can lift and drop the ball behind a line not nearer the hole," said Jimmy. "In that case, his nearest point of relief would be Honolulu."

●

*I*t's hard to estimate Demaret's role in the growth of golf's popularity. He was naturally gregarious and genuinely loved people.

He was scheduled to appear on the old game show "What's My Line?" and was given strict orders to use a specific elevator en route to the studio. Naturally, given a free afternoon prior to the show, he looked up his old friends at "Toots" Shor's bar, and by the time it came to leave for the show he had completely forgotten about something as trivial as an elevator. That he remembered the show at all is remarkable enough.

His appearance set a show record for speed, since he had managed to introduce himself to half the panelists in the elevator on the way to the studio.

At the close of his playing career, Demaret joined with 1956 Masters and PGA Champion Jackie Burke in developing a number of courses, most prominently the Champions course in their hometown, Houston. The Demaret-Burke friendship went back to Jack's childhood, as Demaret liked to explain.

"Jack's dad was a pro in Houston, and we were good friends," said Jimmy. "One night he asked me to baby-sit for Jackie. I agreed, but damned if I knew I was going to be doing it for thirty-five years."

Burke looked at the relationship a little differently. "We Burkes just like to say that Jimmy's been on the payroll all those years."

●

Jimmy Demaret's start in professional golf was hardly auspicious. He left his hometown, Houston, in 1935, with his clubs, his car, and $600 in cash fronted by a nightclub owner, a bandleader, and an oilman.

On his way through Juarez, he managed to get into a game of high-stakes pool.

First he lost the car.

Then he lost the clubs.

Then he lost the $600.

He did manage to hang onto his pawn ticket, which he sent to his brother, who retrieved the clubs and sent them west. The rest, as they say, is history.

BOB DRUM

*"If I had known he was going to grow up and become
Arnold Palmer, I would have been nicer to the bum."*
—Bob Drum, on his reaction to Arnold Palmer after
covering him in a junior tournament in Pennsylvania

Dan Jenkins calls Bob Drum "the Man Who Invented
Arnold Palmer."

Everyone else calls him "the Drummer."

When Drum was in the army (the mind boggles at the
thought) a sergeant took one look and said, "Drum. It's a
perfect name for you. Big, loud, and empty."

But the Drummer is utterly unique. As a writer for the
Pittsburgh Press, he covered Arnold Palmer during his
glory years. In fact, he's sometimes given credit for inspir-
ing Palmer's final-round 65 at Cherry Hills in Denver,
when he won the 1960 U.S. Open.

One version of the story has Palmer talking to Drum
and Dan Jenkins in the locker room before the afternoon's
final round. Palmer asks what would happen if he drove
the first green, eagled the hole, and went on to shoot, say,
a 65.

"Nothing," says Drum. "You're too far back."

"The hell I am," says Palmer. "A 65 gives me 280, and that wins the Open."

"Yeah, when Hogan shoots it," Drum replies. "You got no chance."

Palmer, suitably riled, drives the first green, birdies the hole, shoots 65, and wins the Open.

That's one version, the one told by the Drummer. The other version is about the same, only Jenkins is the one goading Palmer. Either way, the fact of the matter is that both of them were around when golf history was being made—just as they've been for the past half century.

The Drummer enjoyed an all-too-brief career as a feature commentator for CBS Sports with his "Drummer's Beat." One night, while CBS's expense money was weighing down his pockets, he proved why he's one of the best hang-around guys in the game.

"I'll have a Count [Smirnoff] and a glass of milk," he said to the bartender at the Sawgrass Beach Club while ordering a round for all his friends. I asked him what the hell the milk was for.

"You've got to foam the runway," he said.

The Drummer bought a lot of drinks that night. "I have to," he said. "I got to take care of all the guys who took care of me before I was famous."

●

One time George Low, the ultimate hang-around guy in golf, was down on his luck and had to spend a few nights with the Drummer. Someone asked him what it was like.

"It's all right if you don't mind taking a shower with your money in your hand."

*O*ne of the perils of professional journalism as it's practiced around golf courses is that the pressrooms are generally located within walking distance of the grill-rooms. This, plus the facts that tournaments are always being sponsored by beer companies and that so much legwork must, through necessity, be done in bars at night, has been known to take its toll on the press.

On one occasion a friend of the Drummer's decided the time had come to go away and dry out for a while. He asked Bob to come by and drive him to the airport. Since they had some time to kill, and since Drummer's friend was going to be drying out anyway, they decided to have a farewell pop. Or two. Or three.

Well, before you could say "Now boarding at gate number . . . ," the Drummer had decided to make the flight with his friend. Not taking any chances, he called ahead to the clinic.

"There're going to be two drunks getting off the plane," he told the operator at the clinic, in a voice that sounded like a 6′5″ Waring blender. "Keep the little drunk and throw the big drunk back."

●

*O*nce, during his glorious employ by the *Pittsburgh Press*, he asked to go to the British Open to cover Palmer, who was not yet the Arnie America would come to know and love. That being the case, and Pittsburgh being a long way from Scotland, his editor refused. This prompted the Drummer to do what he does best, which is just what he damn pleases, so off he went.

As luck would have it, Palmer played his way into contention, eventually winning.

His editor wired Drum: "Need a thousand words on Palmer at British Open." The Drummer wired back: "Hope you get it."

PRESIDENT DWIGHT D. EISENHOWER

"Just knowing the man is a member of Augusta National tells me all I need to know about his character."
—Jimmy Demaret, on whether he planned to vote for
Ike for president

*T*here have been other presidents of the United States who played golf, but none played it with the passion that President Eisenhower brought to the game. He had a putting green built outside the Oval Office. He was a member of Augusta National, and photos of Ike playing with the best golfers of the era were common in the newspapers of his presidential era.

•

*L*ike many presidents, Eisenhower was a member at Burning Tree, the exclusive club in the Maryland suburbs, and enjoyed getting out for a round to help ease the pressures of the presidency.

One day at Burning Tree, Ike struggled more than usual. The worse he played, the faster his swing became. His caddie tried to be helpful.

"Slow down, baldy," he said.

Things went from bad to worse.

"C'mon, baldy, just slow it down," his caddie implored.

Finally all this got to be too much for the president's playing companions. One of them motioned the caddie aside.

"See here, that's the President of the United States you're talking to," he said to the caddie.

The caddie tried to make up for the error of his ways on Ike's next good shot.

"That's the way to hit it, President Lincoln," he said.

●

S am Snead played a fair amount of golf with Ike, and on one occasion the president was complaining that he'd lost distance off his tee shots.

"Well, Mr. President," said Sam, "you're not turning. You've got to get your ass into the shot."

●

O n one occasion Ike teamed with Bob Hope in a match with General Omar Bradley and Senator Stuart Symington and wound up losing $4. Hope had played badly, so the following day the President took General Bradley as a partner in a match with Hope and Senator Prescott Bush, the father of President Bush. This time Hope played much better, shooting a 75.

As the president paid off his debt, he glared at Hope. "Why didn't you play like this yesterday?" he asked.

*T*he President's love of golf wasn't lost on the Democrats. During the 1956 elections bumper stickers appeared saying, "Ben Hogan for President: If We're Going to Have a Golfer in the White House, Make Him a Good One."

EXCUSES

*P*erhaps no other human endeavor has ever produced the quantity and quality of excuses that golf has. Bad backs, bad marriages, bad ice, you name it—at some time or another every golfer has summoned the reserves of imagination to explain the utter collapse of his or her game.

The best excuse I've ever heard came from a man who shot a horrible qualifying round for the U.S. Open. The USGA requires golfers who fail to score within ten shots of par in the Open qualifying round to send an explanation for their score.

The man wrote that he had been playing very well and made the turn right around par. As he walked down the 10th fairway his son, who was caddying for him, said he had something very important to discuss.

"Not now, son," said the player, but his son was insistent.

"All right, go ahead," said the player. "Tell me what's so important."

"Dad, I'm gay," said his son.

The USGA, in its infinite wisdom, decided that was an acceptable excuse.

MAURICE FLITCROFT

*I*f you have never heard of Maurice Flitcroft, don't feel too bad. He was never a great player. He was never even remotely mediocre. In fact, he could only charitably be described as a golfer. Still, he was one of the biggest stories of the 1976 British Open.

Flitcroft, a crane driver from Barrow-in-Furness, claimed he was a professional and, given the less-than-rigorous standards of the day, was given a spot in the Open qualifying at Formby, where he promptly fired an immaculate 121. Given Flitcroft's training in the game, which was limited to knocking balls around a local beach, this should not have been surprising.

The plucky Flitcroft got off to a shaky start, going 11-12 on the opening holes, scores attributed as much to his scorer's generosity of spirit as his particular skills.

"At the start I was trying too hard," he explained. "By the end of the round I felt I was finally beginning to put it all together."

As indeed he was. His card read 61-60.

His remarkable display triggered a frenzy among the British press, which tracked down Flitcroft's dear mother.

"I've called about Maurice and the Open Championship," stated one reporter.

"Oh my, yes," she replied. "Has he won?"

When told the sad truth, she remained loyal if not upbeat.

"Well, the boy has got to start somewhere, hasn't he?" she replied, as only a mother could.

Moving along, some fourteen years later the amazing Flitcroft—after attempts at entering as an American named Gene Pacecky and as Switzerland's Gerald Hoppy—surfaced at the Open qualifying at Ormskirk, Lancashire, in 1990 and, alas, did not fare very much better. Entered as one James Beau Jolley from France, Flitcroft, now well into his sixties and disguised with dyed hair, a green balaclava, and a moustache, opened with a double bogey and a bogey and, given the contortions of his swing, was soon escorted from the course by an official.

Still, despite the indignity of it all, Flitcroft was not apologetic in the least: "I have always believed in my potential, but I was not warmed up properly," he explained.

IVAN GANTZ

*T*ake a stroll through the history books and you'll be hard pressed to find many mentions of Ivan Gantz. Still, in his own way, he is every bit as legendary as Snead, Hogan, Nicklaus, or the rest—of course, Ivan Gantz's own way wasn't anything they'd teach you in a golf school.

"People always said I had a temper, but those little dudes never caught a glimpse of Ivan the Terrible," Tommy Bolt once said. "He used to warm up before a round, and before he'd even tee off he was throwing clubs on the practice range. He used to have a habit of stomping on his driver when he hit a bad shot. His driver looked like a bunch of termites had gotten loose all over it. One time I was paired with him, and he was the last to drive. He hit, I started walking down the fairway, and I heard him yelling back from the tee, 'Help, help!' I looked back, and there he was hobbling down the fairway with his driver stuck to the bottom of his shoe. Oh, Ivan was a beauty."

A s if wreaking havoc upon his clubs wasn't enough, Gantz was also widely noted for beating the hell out of himself. Once, in a tournament, Don January saw Gantz in an adjacent fairway, bleeding heavily from his nose. It turned out that Gantz had missed a putt on the previous green and bashed himself severely with the offending blade. On another occasion, Jackie Burke says he saw Gantz savagely pounding his head against a tree trunk. Burke wasn't exactly sure what to do, so he simply said hello.

"Hi, pards," said Gantz, who then went back to bashing his head against the tree.

WALTER HAGEN

"I never really wanted to be a millionaire. I just wanted to live like one."

—Walter Hagen

"The thing about Walter is, he wouldn't spend your money any faster than he'd spend his own."

—Bob Harlow, golf promoter

*T*he Great Haig was one of the dominant—and most colorful—golfers of the 1910s and 1920s. A brilliant player, he was also a showman who did much to popularize the game. Hagen liked to party, although not as much as his reputation allowed. He won two U.S. and four British Opens (becoming the first American to win the title), as well as five PGA championships. He was awesome in the PGA, which was a match play event until 1958. Hagen excelled at match play, where he could bring the full force of his game—and gamesmanship—into play.

For all his wins and notoriety, Hagen is perhaps best known for his philosophy: "Life is much too short. Make sure to take time and smell the flowers along the way."

O n the eve of the PGA finals in 1926 a friend ran into Hagen at a party around midnight.

"My God, Walter, what are you doing up?" he asked. "Leo [Diegel, his opponent] has been in bed since eight o'clock."

"Yes," said Hagen, "But he hasn't been sleeping."

Sure enough, in the next day's match, Hagen made a point of giving Diegel—a mediocre putter at best—every early short putt. Then at a crucial point in the match he dropped the other shoe. Diegel, faced with a short putt for a tie, looked to Hagen to see if he would give him the putt. Hagen looked Diegel straight in the eyes and said nothing. Diegel's putt never came close to the hole. And he was never again in the match.

•

H agen was the nonplaying captain of the American team in the 1937 Ryder Cup matches in Southport, England. Anxious to praise all the appropriate figures, he had made extensive notes but unfortunately lost them before he reached the presentation ceremonies. Nevertheless, he persevered.

"You have no idea how honored I am to captain the first American Ryder Cup team to win on home soil . . ."

Several people in the crowd corrected him, pointing out that he meant to say "foreign soil."

"An honest mistake," he said. "You can't blame me for feeling so completely at home over here, now can you?"

*H*agen came to the final green of the 1919 U.S. Open at Brae Burn needing to make a testing putt to force a playoff with Mike Brady. After surveying the putt from every angle, he asked, "Where's Mike?" He wanted to make sure that Brady saw him make the putt so Brady would have something to think about as he tossed and turned that night—when Hagen would most certainly be sleeping.

In the playoff Hagen displayed his keen knowledge of both the rules and human nature. Just prior to teeing off, he suggested that the heavily muscled Brady roll his shirtsleeves down.

"Why?" asked Brady.

"So the gallery won't see your muscles shaking," Hagen replied.

The match proceeded along closely until the 17th hole, when Hagen drove his ball into a bunker, where it plugged in a seam where the face of the bunker had been sodded. The shot was clearly unplayable, and Hagen faced losing a hole at a crucial stage of the match.

But Hagen knew the rules. He insisted that he needed to identify his ball and was allowed a lift to do so, followed by a free drop into a perfect lie. He went on to par the hole and win the championship by a shot.

●

*H*agen loved parties and celebrities, ideally at the same time. At one Hollywood party he was joined by actor Richard Arlen. When the bill arrived, Arlen insisted upon paying, but Hagen, in a grand gesture, swept the check from the waiter and strolled magnificently to the cashier. While everyone at the table praised Hagen's generosity of wallet and spirit, he blithely signed Arlen's name to the bill and left, a true prince among men.

*H*agen never understood why skilled professionals spent so much time warming up before a round. He'd hit a handful of balls to get a feel. Any more than that was, in his words, "corporal punishment." His philosophy was that he was going to miss six shots a round anyway, most of them early before things got serious.

"The early mistakes are something you have to live with," he explained. "It's the mistakes late in the day that kill you, and I know my game will be in shape by then. Besides, the worst thing that's going to happen is a playoff, and I haven't met the guy who can beat me head-to-head."

●

*H*agen met Joe Turnesa in the finals of the 1927 PGA Championship in Dallas. He arrived a half hour late, apologized grandly, and proceeded to tank the first three holes of the match, giving Turnesa a three-up lead in match play.

"There, Joe," he said, standing on the 4th tee. "That makes up for the half hour you had to wait. Now we'll play."

And so they did. When they came to the 18th, the match was even. Hagen hit a poor drive, and his approach from the tall grass was hindered by a stand of tall trees. Turnesa, in the center of the fairway, watched helplessly as Hagen walked back and forth, pulled a variety of different clubs from the bag, checked the wind, dillied and dallied for as long as possible, and finally announced grandly that he had only the slimmest of chances of pulling off a "miracle shot"—which, of course, he did, leaving the ball twelve feet from the hole.

Turnesa, his concentration hopelessly lost, dumped his approach into a bunker and lost the title, one-up.

*H*agen faced Leo Diegel in the finals of the 1926 PGA Championship. Diegel was an intense, nervous player with a questionable putting stroke at best. In other words, a perfect opponent for Hagen.

After the morning round, Hagen invited Diegel to join him for lunch. Diegel forced down some light tea and toast and watched in horror as Hagen dined on vichyssoise and roast duck washed down by champagne. This was too much for Diegel, who fell sick to his stomach and raced from the table, colliding with a glass door along the way. Hagen won the championship, 5 and 3.

●

*H*agen loved the British, but he had a field day tweaking the noses of their institutions.

Once, while playing a celebrated round with the Prince of Wales (who would go on to be best known for giving up the British throne for American divorcée Wallis Simpson), he asked, "Eddie, hold the flagstick while I putt this one, will you?"

On another occasion he arrived at the 1920 British Open in a magnificent Austro-Daimler limousine. When he tried to enter the clubhouse, he was informed that professionals were restricted to the professional's shop. Hagen would do no such thing. He ordered his chauffeur to park the limo in front of the clubhouse, in full view of the members, where he was served a full lunch, including expensive wines, each day by his footman.

When in 1922 he won the British Open at Royal St. George's, he made a grand gesture of turning over his winner's check of 50 British pounds directly to his caddie, who, it is said, never recovered from such generosity and drank himself into an early oblivion.

*L*ike many players of earlier eras, Hagen made most of his money from exhibitions, which suited him perfectly as he adored travel and loved to see how rich guys around the world lived.

Following one such tour that netted him a colossal $23,000, he was forced to stay in his San Francisco hotel room for three days because he'd squandered all his money and couldn't afford to get his clothes out of the cleaners.

●

*H*agen's love of life clearly extended to women. As Lady Bird Johnson once said about her husband, the late president, "Lyndon loved people, and half the people in the world just happen to be women." So it was with Hagen.

One evening, at a formal dinner in New York, he was introduced to Ernestine Schumann-Heink, a famous contralto with the Metropolitan Opera. Her notoriety did not impress him nearly as much as her figure.

"My dear," he said, gazing down at her low-cut evening gown, "did you ever stop and think what a wonderful bunker you would make?"

CLAYTON HEAFNER

*"Clayton was the most even-tempered golfer I ever saw.
He was mad all the time."*

—Sam Snead

*O*ne year Clayton had it going pretty good in Oakland
until he hit a shot that wound up stuck in a tree,"
Jimmy Demaret once recalled. "Now Clayton was a big
man, well over two-hundred-fifty pounds. He climbed up
in that tree and punched the ball out, but by that time he
was pretty much out of control. The next year he arrived
on the first tee, and the announcer introduced him as
'Clayton Heefner from Linville, North Carolina.' That was
bad enough, but to make matters worse the announcer
said he hoped that Clayton wouldn't have any problems
with Oakland's trees this time. The crowd thought that
was pretty funny, but not Clayton.

" 'My name is Heafner, not Heefner,' he said to the
gallery. 'I'm from Charlotte, not Linville. And as for staying out of your trees, I'm not even going to give myself a
chance to get in them. C'mon, boy, stick that stuff in the
car.' And with that he packed up and headed for San
Francisco."

As a young man Charlie Price, the gifted writer, tried his hand on the tour without—as he'll be the first to admit—much notable success. Finally he asked Clayton Heafner for some advice.

"Charlie," said Heafner, "did you notice that all the guys doing well out here are built like truck drivers, but they have the touch of hairdressers? Well, you're built like a hairdresser, and you have the touch of a truck driver."

BEN HOGAN

"People are always wondering who's better, Hogan or Nicklaus. Well, I've seen Jack Nicklaus watch Ben practice, but I've never seen Ben watch anybody else practice. What's that tell you?"

—Tommy Bolt

*F*ew golfers ever aspired to, and achieved, the degree of perfection or played with the cold, ruthless intensity of Ben Hogan.

Australia's five-time British Open Champion Peter Thomson called Hogan "the standard of excellence against which we all measured ourselves."

Sam Snead, Hogan's greatest rival, always claimed that he enjoyed playing against Hogan. "The whole point of the game is to go up against the best players. When I was able to beat Ben, I knew I had beaten the best."

It was typical of Hogan that when in 1953 he started his equipment company he wrote to club professionals pledging that his clubs would be made to the highest standards. When the first line of irons came out, he ordered them destroyed. One of his partners protested, arguing that it would cost the company hundreds of thousands of dollars. For Hogan it was a matter of his reputation, not dollars and cents, so he bought out his partner and destroyed the $150,000 worth of clubs.

71

*I*t is entirely possible that except for a single round in the 1938 Oakland Open, the world would never have heard of Ben Hogan.

He first tried the tour—such as it was in those days— in 1932 but without success. He'd run out of money and return to Fort Worth, where he'd find a series of odd jobs that would give him a stake and also enough time to work on his game. This happened time and again.

"Ben was a good enough player, but he had a long swing—too long for his size," remembers Sam Snead. "He'd put together a few good rounds and then throw a 77 up on the board. That would just kill him."

He married in 1935 and tried the tour again in 1937, but by the time he and his wife reached Oakland in 1938 they had been living on candy bars and fruit, were staying in the cheapest hotel in town, and had only $8 to their name. Unless a miracle happened, Ben and Valerie Hogan were heading home to Fort Worth for good.

"The tournament was played at the Claremont Country Club, and when I arrived I remember seeing Ben standing outside, banging his fists against a brick wall, as close to tears as I ever saw him," says Snead. "A couple of us asked him what was wrong. We thought something had happened to Valerie.

" 'I can't go on,' Ben said. 'Some son of a bitch stole the tires off my car last night. I'm finished.'

"Well, Ben went out that day, and he was as grim as anyone you'd ever seen. I believe he shot a 69 to finish second to Harry Cooper. He made almost $400, and that kept him going. He never looked back after that."

Hogan would later say that round and that check meant more to him than anything else he ever accomplished in golf.

*W*hen Hogan won the 1950 U.S. Open at Merion, he did it without a 7-iron in his bag for the four rounds of regulation play. When reporters asked him why, he gave an answer that spoke volumes about his mastery of course management.

"There isn't a 7-iron shot at Merion," he said.

Coming to the 72nd hole of regulation play, Hogan laced a magnificent 1-iron approach that Cary Middlecoff called the "purest stroke I've ever seen," then went on to make his par.

At some point following his round, the 1-iron was stolen, and Hogan replaced it with his 7-iron. Some thirty years later, a collector found a 1-iron bearing Hogan's name and a worn area about the size of a dime on the clubface, perilously close to the hosel. He figured, rightly, that it had to be the missing 1-iron. He sent it to Hogan, who confirmed that it was and then gave it to the U.S. Golf Association for their collection of his memorabilia.

●

*H*ogan and his wife, Valerie, were in Los Angeles for the 1937 Los Angeles Open. One night in their hotel room Valerie sat and watched her husband work on his putting, which he considered the weakest part of his game. Finally she offered some advice.

"Ben, I know the solution to your putting problems," she said.

"Well, would you be so good as to let me know?" he replied.

"All you have to do is hit the ball closer to the hole," she said.

I was lucky when I came out on tour because I would play a lot of my practice rounds with Ben, and I never failed to learn something from him," recalls Ken Venturi. "Ben wouldn't always teach you, in the strict sense, but he expected you to be able to learn through observing. Once, at Southern Hills for the 1958 Open, we were playing a practice round. He told me, 'Whatever you do, don't miss this green to the right.'

"I thought I could read a hole pretty well, but I couldn't see any real trouble to the right, so I asked what the danger was over there.

" 'That's where the players will walk to the next tee,' Ben said. 'They'll trample the grass down and you'll be pitching back against the grain in the rough. That's too tough a shot.'

"People often ask what Ben's secret was," says Kenny. "I'd say he was just that much smarter and more observant than the rest of the field; plus, he outworked them."

●

B en was incredibly precise," recalls Gardner Dickinson, a Hogan protégé who once surreptitiously gave Hogan an IQ test (Dickinson was trained in clinical psychology) and concluded that he ranked at the genius level. "Before Ben started his own company he was under contract with MacGregor. He'd play their clubs, but he didn't like their ball and wouldn't play it. Finally one of the company guys tried to convince Ben by arguing that their testing machine had proven that their ball was superior. Ben told them that if he couldn't hit the ball better than their machine he'd quit golf.

"He used to get shipments of balls and go over them with a magnifying glass," Dickinson continues. "Every so often he'd reject one because there was too much paint in the dimples. Now that is precise."

*B*en was playing with Claude Harmon in the Masters one year," recalls Sam Snead. "They came to the par 3 12th, which is one of the toughest holes in the world. Claude made a hole-in-one, and the crowd went crazy. Ben made a two, and as they walked off the green he said to Claude, 'You know, Claude, I can't remember the last time I made a two there. What did you make?'

" 'Why Ben, I made an ace,' said Claude.

" 'Oh, well, that's great, Claude,' he said, as he headed off to the next tee.

"That was just Ben's way. He didn't mean anything by it. He just got into his own world out there, and that was that. I always liked to play with Ben. He played his game and let you play yours."

•

*H*ogan and his wife, Valerie, were returning home to Fort Worth from Phoenix on a foggy morning, February 2, 1949, when they collided with a Greyhound bus that was trying to pass a slow-moving truck. Hogan instinctively threw himself across the front seat to protect his wife, an act that saved his life since it kept him from being impaled by the steering column.

Still, he was shattered by the accident. He had suffered a broken pelvis, shoulder, rib, and ankle. He was in severe shock and had suffered considerable blood loss. In the hospital he was placed in a cast from his chest to his knees. A month later when the cast was removed, a blood clot was discovered, leaving doctors no choice but to tie off the vena cava, a large vein in the leg that returns blood to the heart.

Nobody expected Hogan to play golf, let alone tournament golf, again. There was some doubt whether he'd even be able to walk. But those who saw Hogan in those early days after the accident caught a glimpse of the man's indomitable spirit.

Because of the effects of the crash and the medication, Hogan would have periods of delirium in which he would unconsciously grip and regrip an imaginary club. At other times he would seem to be tossing blades of grass into the air to check the wind. On occasion he would motion with his left arm, calling "Back on the left, please, back on the left," trying to clear a gallery that existed only in his mind.

●

*T*he 1951 Ryder Cup matches were played at Pine-hurst in North Carolina. One day Max Faulkner, a member of the British side, happened to be watching Hogan practicing.

"I say, Ben, I believe I could help you with a bit of advice on that fade of yours. If you'd drop your right hand a bit under the shaft, you'd cure your fade."

"You don't see the caddie moving any, do you?" replied Hogan icily.

●

*H*ogan traveled to Carnoustie, Scotland, for the 1953 British Open. It would be the only time he played in the championship, and he won it, earning a ticker-tape parade when he sailed back to New York City.

Carnoustie was unlike any course he had ever seen. When asked for his impression of the course he said, "I've got a lawn mower back home in Texas. I'll send it over."

*H*ogan does have a fine sense of humor, but it is rarely displayed to those he doesn't know well. Tommy Bolt was a good friend and credited him with helping develop his game. They played together often. On one occasion, they came to the difficult 176-yard, par 3, 16th at Colonial Country Club in Hogan's hometown, Fort Worth.

"We got into a friendly argument about which was the right club. I said it was a 5-iron, Ben insisted it was a 4. We put a little wager down, and I hit first, putting it in there about twenty feet. Ben took his damned 4-iron and put it inside me.

" 'See, Tommy, it was a 4,' Ben said.

" 'But you hit it fat, Ben,' I said.

" 'Yes, but the shot called for a fat 4,' he said."

●

*B*eginning in 1990, the Ben Hogan company sponsored The Hogan Tour for players unable either to get on or stay on the PGA Tour. A reporter asked Ben Hogan what advice he'd have for struggling young players:

"Watch out for buses," Hogan said.

●

*O*nce while playing an exhibition, Hogan faced a long, difficult shot. Since he was unfamiliar with the course, he asked the caddie what he had to the green.

"Everything you've got," said the caddie.

"How do you know what everything I have is?" replied Hogan.

*A*s is their regular practice during the Colonial Invitational, CBS's Frank Chirkinian and Ken Venturi arranged to meet Ben Hogan for lunch at his club, Shady Oaks. Gary McCord, a CBS announcer and tour player, asked if he could stop by and meet Hogan. When he arrived, he was introduced to Hogan, who pondered the name.

"McCord, McCord," he puzzled. "What did you do before you were an announcer?"

"Well, Mr. Hogan, I've played the tour for fifteen years," said McCord.

"What did you ever win?" Hogan asked.

"Nothing, Mr. Hogan," said McCord.

"Well, why are you still out there?" Hogan asked.

"I don't know," answered McCord.

"I don't know either," said Hogan. "Would you like a drink?"

●

*J*immy Demaret always said that people never gave Ben credit for being as good a bunker player as he was, because they never saw him in one," recalls Dave Marr. "I was working at Seminole as an assistant to Claude Harmon, and Ben used to come down to prepare for the Masters. One day Ben, Claude, and Chris Dunphy got to playing call shots from a bunker, and Ben pulled out his 4-wood. He was just unbelievable. People talk about Seve being a magician with a 2-iron from the sand, but Ben was every bit as good. He just wore those guys out, and if you don't think that's hard, you just go take your 4-wood into a bunker and give it a try."

*T*oday most golfers play strictly by the numbers. Both pros and amateurs check the yardage to the hole before they make their club selection, and never mind that most of us don't really have a clue how far we really hit each club.

In Hogan's day, however, it was a different game. People played by sight and made their club selections based on the shot they envisioned. Depending on the lie, the wind, the configuration of the green, and the humidity, a player might pull almost any club in the bag. Here's a case in point. One day Hogan was playing with an assistant professional—a talented player—from a club in Dallas. The pro repeatedly asked Hogan what he would hit from a given spot. Finally Hogan, facing an approach from 150 yards out, gave the ultimate playing lesson. He emptied all the balls from his bag and hit the green with each club—except his putter.

●

*O*ne year Hogan was paired with a talented young player in the Colonial Invitational. On the first hole, the young player hit his approach inside Hogan.

"You're away, I believe, Mr. Hogan," the player said.

The same thing happened on the second hole. On the fourth hole, a 226-yard par 3, the player hit a good drive. Hogan selected his club, made a good swing, and just after impact—without even looking at the flight of the ball—said "You're away."

HOWARD HUGHES

*F*ew people realize that as a young man Howard Hughes was a very good player. He was constantly taking lessons from Willie Hunter at Riviera Country Club in Los Angeles and is said to have taken a lesson every day for three months straight at one point. But as good as he was, one day he did what millions of golfers have threatened to do but can't: he quit.

One day at Bel-Air he played with George Von Elm, the former U.S. Amateur champion who lost to Billy Burke in a 36-hole playoff for the 1931 U.S. Open.

"George," he asked, "do you think I'm good enough to win the U.S. Amateur?"

"Qualify for it? Maybe. Win it? No," Von Elm replied.

Hughes got up and left . . . and never played golf again.

He did, however, get his retribution by crash-landing a plane on one of the fairways at Bel-Air, which proves that while no one—even the wealthiest among us—can bring the game to its knees, it is possible to get a measure of revenge now and again.

BOBBY JONES

*"As a young man he was able to stand up to just about
the best that life can offer, which is not easy, and later he
stood up, with equal grace, to just about the worst."*
—Herbert Warren Wind

*F*irst, consider the record: when Bob Jones retired
from championship play in 1930, at the age of just
twenty-eight, he had won four U.S. Opens, three British
Opens, five U.S. Amateurs, and a British Amateur.

But perhaps more impressive, if indeed that is possible,
is the fact that even now, almost twenty years after his
death in 1971, he remains the standard against which
golf's champions are measured, both as players and as
gentlemen. He is the ideal.

Jones's later years were lived out in a tragic battle
against the degenerative nerve disease syringomyelia,
which wasted his body and confined him to a wheelchair.
But yet, like President Kennedy, he seems a figure frozen
in time. To remember Bob Jones is to see him in plus
fours, shirt, and tie with Calamity Jane, his putter, at
hand.

*I*n 1953, after winning the Masters and the U.S. and British Opens, Ben Hogan was honored at a dinner hosted by the USGA in New York. At the height of Hogan's career, it was only natural that people should compare him with Jones—but Jones would have no part of it. When asked if he thought he would have beaten Hogan, Jones displayed both his grace and intelligence by answering, "I don't know. I never played him. But I'm not one who believes my era was the greatest necessarily because I played in it."

●

*B*en Crenshaw was once asked who his ideal dinner companion would be. He said "Bob Jones, and not necessarily because of his golf."

●

*I*n the 1925 U.S. Open at Worcester (Massachusetts) Country Club, Jones called a penalty upon himself, stating that his ball had moved when he addressed it. Nobody but Jones had seen the ball move, and the ensuing one-stroke penalty put him into a playoff with Willie Macfarlane, who beat him the next day.

Later, when Jones was praised for his sportsmanship, he bristled.

"There's only one way to play the game," he said. "You might as well praise a man for not robbing a bank as to praise him for playing by the rules."

*B*ob Jones came to symbolize the best in sportsman-ship, but that isn't to say he didn't have a temper early in his career. In the 1921 British Open, Jones got his first glimpse of St. Andrews, a course he grew to love above all others. But in the final round he shot himself out of contention with a 46 on the front 9, took a double bogey on the 10th, then made a five on the par 3 11th. This was too much for the young man. He put his ball in his pocket, tore up his card, cast it to the wind, and then walked in.

Jones, of whom so much was expected, was severely criticized on both sides of the Atlantic. That criticism grew worse when, in the U.S. Amateur, he threw a club after a poor shot. The club hit a spectator, and while it didn't do any damage, it prompted a severe reprimand from the USGA, warning him that any more displays of temper would lead to a ban from any further national competitions. It was a ban that was never mentioned again.

●

*I*t's a misconception that Jones came from a wealthy family, as so many top amateurs of his era did. In fact, he came from a family of comfortable means, and when he retired from competition at age twenty-eight, he set about to earn a living. And he was well aware of his market value, as Ferris Mack, an editor at Doubleday, learned when he called Jones with a book proposal. Jones liked the idea, and when the subject came around to money, Mack told Jones that the advance would be $10,000—a healthy sum in those days. Mack's offer met with silence, and then Jones replied in his measured southern drawl: "Ferris, I don't cross the damn street for $10,000."

*I*n 1925 Jones met Watts Gunn in the finals of the U.S. Amateur at Oakmont. This marked the only time two members of the same club have met in the finals.

As luck would have it, Gunn met a young lady from Pittsburgh and was quite taken. The evening before the final, he made plans to meet her but ran into Jones as he was making his way down a back stairway. Jones, who had talked Gunn's parents into letting their son make the trip from Atlanta, stopped Gunn in his tracks.

"Oh, no you don't," Jones said. "You march right up to that room. You'll need all the sleep you can get for tomorrow."

As it turned out, Gunn could have stayed out all night. Jones beat him, 8 and 7.

●

*U*ntil 1965 the final two rounds of the U.S. Open were played on Saturday. This meant that any playoffs would be held on Sunday. When Bob Jones and Al Espinosa tied in the 1929 Open at Winged Foot, the 36-hole playoff was scheduled to begin early Sunday morning.

Jones, who was a Protestant, realized that an early tee time would prevent Espinosa, a Catholic, from attending Mass. Jones went to the USGA and asked them to set back the starting time. The USGA agreed, and the following morning the Espinosas and the Joneses attended local Catholic services.

Syringomyelia, the disease that eventually killed Bob Jones, was particularly cruel as it ravaged his body while, at the same time, leaving his mind and wit as sharp as ever.

A few years before his death, when he was at the Masters for the final time, a friend stopped by Jones's cabin for a visit. He was shocked by Jones's appearance and was unable to hide his emotions.

"Now, now," said Jones. "We won't have any of that. We must all play the ball as we find it."

●

Just three days before his death in December 1971 Jones confided to a friend, "If I had known it would be this easy, I wouldn't have been so worried about it."

The *New York Times* once summed up his career—and life—by observing that "with dignity, he quit the memorable scene on which he nothing common did, or mean."

ROBERT TRENT JONES

"Trent, I've just seen a course you'd really like. You stand on the first tee and take an unplayable lie."
—Jimmy Demaret

*N*o golf course architect has been as prodigious and, until Pete Dye, as controversial as Robert Trent Jones. He is credited with making course architecture a modern profession and, indeed, a lucrative one. Jones combined an artistic eye with a keen grasp of finances and public relations. As is evidenced in the following story, Trent Jones has a knack of being in the right place at the right time—and making the most of it.

"I was commissioned to modernize the Lower Course at Baltusrol for the 1954 U.S. Open," Jones recalls. "Some of the membership felt I had made the course too difficult, particularly the 4th hole, a 194-yard par 3 over water. Of course, the last thing I wanted was an unhappy membership, so I went over to Baltusrol and played with Johnny Farrell, the professional, C. P. Burgess, the tournament chairman, and another member. When we came to the 4th hole, all three fellows hit the green with their drives. I pulled out a mashie and, as luck would have it, made a hole-in-one. As soon as the ball went into the hole, I turned to my hosts and said, 'Gentlemen, I believe this hole is eminently fair.'"

ALEX KARRAS

S ome sports seem to turn out better golfers than others. For example, hockey players seem to take to the game with a certain ease, as do baseball players, probably because they both have so much free time during the day when the weather is warm. Basketball players are at a disadvantage because of their height. Some football players, by position, seem well suited to the game—quarterbacks John Brodie of the 49ers and Phil Simms of the Giants, for example, or conversely, Alex Karras, the legendary tackle of the Detroit Lions turned actor.

One day Karras stood on the first tee of the Red Run Golf Club in Royal Oak, Michigan, went through all the usual motions, and proceeded to smash a thunderous drive through the clubhouse's huge plate-glass window, which promptly shattered in a roar of splintered glass and decorum.

Karras, suitably embarrassed, walked over the gaping space where the window had once been and asked a startled waiter, "Hey, is this room out of bounds?"

PRESIDENT
JOHN F. KENNEDY

*P*resident Kennedy's love of athletic competition has been well chronicled. What is less well known, largely because Kennedy took pains to hide it from the public that equated golf with President Eisenhower, was that he loved golf and was probably the best player of all America's presidents.

One day when vacationing in Florida he played at Seminole with Chris Dunphy, the club's chairman and an old friend of the Kennedy family. On the first hole Kennedy hit a fine drive and followed it with a 4-iron approach three feet from the hole. When they reached the green Kennedy looked to Dunphy, expecting him to concede the putt to the president.

"C'mon, Chris, certainly you're going to give me this putt," said Kennedy.

"Well, Mr. President, it's still early in the round. Why don't you putt it so I can see what your stroke looks like today?"

"Okay, fine, but let's get going," Kennedy said. "I've got a meeting with the head of the Internal Revenue Service as soon as we finish."

"It's good," said Dunphy, knocking the ball away and heading for the next tee.

TOM KITE

*T*om Kite has graced golf with his dedication and sportsmanship and has been rewarded with the respect of his fellow players, the press, and the galleries. That he has won more money on the PGA Tour than any other player in history is another testament to the strength of his game and character.

Like Jack Nicklaus, he is as gracious in defeat as in victory, which was evidenced following his loss of the 1989 U.S. Open, when he handled the press and the fans with uncommon dignity.

He enjoyed a fine amateur career, but when he told his father that he planned to turn pro and try the tour, his father prescribed a healthy dose of realism.

"Tom, for every one hundred men who try the tour, ninty-nine will fail," said Mr. Kite.

"Dad, I sure feel sorry for those other ninty-nine, because I intend to make it," said Tom.

And make it he has, in a big and well deserved way.

KY LAFFOON

"Drown, you son of a bitch, drown."
—Ky Laffoon, as he repeatedly dunked his putter
in a lake after a poor round

*K*y Laffoon was an enormously talented, if wildly eccentric, professional who played his best golf in the 1930s. He got his start as a caddie for Titanic Thompson, the legendary hustler. Thompson would size up a prospective victim and announce, "Hell, my caddie could beat you," which, of course, Ky Laffoon could—and would.

"People talk about Ky as if he were stupid, but he was actually quite smart," recalled Paul Runyan. "But I will concede that he often did things that would cause you to doubt his intelligence if you didn't know him. Once, in the Sacramento Open, he missed a putt on the final hole. He swung the putter at his foot. Instead of hitting it with the wooden shaft, as he planned, the clubhead struck his toe, breaking both the putter and his toe. He hobbled up to the ball and went to tap the ball in. Of course, since there was no head on the putter, he missed the ball completely, adding a one-stroke insult to injury."

*K*y's wife was a very nice woman who just hated it when Ky would curse," says Sam Snead. "Every now and again, to calm her down, Ky would promise to control his temper and his cussing.

"Everything was going just fine until one tournament when Ky hit his ball into a jungle behind one of the greens. Well, then he started swearing up a blue streak and just raking the hell out of the shrubs and weeds. His wife had heard enough, and she set off a-runnin' for the car, with old Ky hot on her heels. He tried to apologize, but since he also had a stutter when he got excited, it wasn't all that believable.

" 'Honey, I-I-I w-wasn't cussin', honest," he told her. "It didn't have nuthin' to do with the golf. It's j-just that I h-hate honeysuckle.' "

●

*P*eople have heard stories about Ky punishing his clubs and can't believe they are true, but they truly are," recalls Runyan. "In those days we drove from tournament to tournament, and Ky would get in these dark moods after a poor round. It wasn't unusual for him to tie his putter to the rear bumper of his car and drag it along the road to punish it. He'd also open a door and drag a club along the pavement for a few miles, with sparks shooting up all over the place. Of course, in fairness to Ky, he occasionally did that to grind off some of the sole or sharpen the leading edge."

TONY LEMA

*T*ony Lema, who won the 1964 British Open at St. Andrews, was a player of enormous talent, charisma, and potential who died in a plane crash in 1966. Lema's win at St. Andrews was remarkable for two reasons: first, it was his first British Open; and second, he only played one practice round and didn't finish that. Working (literally) in his favor was Tip Anderson, Arnold Palmer's longtime Scottish caddie, on loan to Lema that week.

●

*W*e had just finished playing in Akron," recalls Ken Venturi, who grew up in San Francisco, across the bay from Tony. "Tony was supposed to stay for a dinner, but he got this offer to fly to Chicago for an outing. I felt I could be pretty honest with him, so I told him he was making a mistake by skipping out on the people in Akron. My exact words were 'You'll regret doing this the rest of your life.' Even today I can't get over how eerie those words still sound."

JACK LEMMON

"Now here's Jack Lemmon, about to play the all-important eighth shot. . . ."
—ABC's Jim McKay, reporting on play at Pebble Beach's
14th hole in the 1959 Crosby

*F*ew golfers bring as much enthusiasm to the game as Jack Lemmon. The annual telecast of the AT&T is an exercise in high drama because of Lemmon's attempts (almost certainly in vain) to play well enough to be around for Sunday's final round. Still, what he lacks in skill he more than makes up in his sheer love of the game.

One year, in yet another one of his valiant efforts to get his team into contention, he suffered perhaps the ultimate indignity.

"There I was, pretty much out of it again, but I knew the cameras were on me, so I wanted to make a decent showing coming in," Lemmon recalls. "I had a putt for— I don't know—a double or triple bogey, and as I was lining it up I turned to my caddie and asked him how he thought it would break.

" 'Who cares?' he answered.

"I couldn't really get mad," says Lemmon. "He had a good point."

LAWSON LITTLE

*L*awson Little won the U.S. and British Amateur championships in 1934 and 1935 and went on to win the 1940 U.S. Open at Canterbury in a playoff with Gene Sarazen. But Little's win was not without its trying moments—moments that provide a valuable lesson for those who would forget that the golf swing is an athletic movement and not the second coming of the lunar lander.

Lawson took the early lead in their playoff, but on the 5th hole a fan approached and politely wondered if he might ask Little a question. Little, an outgoing and affable man, told him to go right ahead.

"I was just wondering whether you inhale or exhale on your backswing?" he asked.

"Are you serious?" Little asked.

"Oh, quite," said the man. "For myself, I think I inhale, but I'm not sure."

Hook, hook, hook was Little's reply as his swing broke down under the enormous weight of trying to figure out his breathing patterns.

HENRY LONGHURST

*F*or some forty-five years Henry Longhurst wrote a
weekly golf column for the *Sunday Times* of London
as well as articles on a wide variety of subjects for publi-
cations all over the world. He was best known in America
for his writing in *Golf Digest* and for his work as an
announcer for CBS and ABC on their golf telecasts.

Having cut his television teeth, so to speak, with the
BBC, he was scarcely a newcomer when CBS's Frank
Chirkinian put him on a tower during the 1965 Carling
Tournament in Sutton, Massachusetts. He caused some-
thing of a sensation by observing that a topped 2-iron by
Homero Blancas was "quite a terrible one, right off the
bottom of the club. Terrible."

On another occasion he was assigned to the par 3 16th
at Augusta National. After watching yet another player's
demise on Sunday, he said simply, "Pity," and went on
about his business.

Longhurst, like all golf writers, was constantly being
offered trips to exotic locales—free, of course—to look at
the latest in a long line of "championship" courses blight-
ing the landscape. Longhurst happily took up many of
these offers but had a word of caution for those who
would follow in his footsteps.

"Lads," he'd say, "enjoy their women, drink their whis-
key, welcome their hospitality in every form, but never,

under any circumstances, write so much as a word about their bloody awful courses."

●

*L*onghurst fought a courageous battle with cancer before his death on July 21, 1978. In his last piece, written three weeks before his death, he wrote, "To me golf has brought a congenial life, as I hope these pages may have shown: a life spent among pleasant people, who have mostly been at their own pleasantest in the circumstances in which I have met them, often at some of the great beauty spots of the world.

"Now it is time to lay down my pen and, alas, the microphone, too, and to reflect, in whatever time may be left, how uncommonly lucky I have been. And if I have managed to give a little pleasure along the way, well, what a happy thought that is, too."

JOE LOUIS

When the heavyweight champion of the world hung up his gloves he picked up his clubs and turned pro. While he played in a few PGA Tour events, he spent most of his time on the old Negro Tour, where there were a number of good players who could have made it on the PGA Tour but were kept out by an exclusionary clause in the PGA bylaws.

One day Louis came to the final hole in a match with Ted Rhodes, one of the top players on the Negro Tour.

"How far am I from the hole?" Louis asked his caddie.

"Champ, you're a bogey away and a $10 bill to Mr. Ted," came the reply.

DAVIS LOVE, JR.

*D*avis Love, Jr., was a man of uncommon insight, patience, and gentle humor who combined these qualities with an unsurpassed knowledge of golf and a passion for teaching. He had enjoyed some success on tour but ultimately gave up playing at that level to devote himself to teaching and to his family. His son, Davis III, joined the tour after a fine amateur career and has won twice.

Davis Love, Jr., died in a 1988 plane crash along with a pilot and two other teachers, Jimmy Hodges and John Poppa.

●

*I*n 1960 Davis showed up at Winged Foot to try to qualify for the U.S. Open. Earlier he had slashed open a six-stitch cut in his right forefinger. This prevented him from hitting down with his iron shots, so he put together a set of lofted woods that would allow him to sweep the ball from the fairway, sparing his finger additional injury.

Before Love teed off, an official took one look at his hand and urged him to withdraw, saying that it was obvious that he couldn't possibly play. The thought of pulling out had crossed his mind, but there was something in the official's tone that bothered Love. Determined to prove the man wrong, Love fought his way around the course, qualifying for the Open at Cherry Hills.

Once there, he shot a first round 74 but tore open his finger in the second round, shooting another 74 and missing the cut by a shot.

●

*D*avis Love once found himself paired with Lee Trevino in the PGA Championship. Love was an extremely nervous player who had to keep to himself, blocking out any distractions in order to play well.

"Lee," he said, as they were leaving the first tee, "I'm pretty nervous, so if it's all the same to you, I don't think I'll do much talking."

"That's okay, Davis," said Trevino. "All you have to do is listen. I'll do enough talking for both of us."

GEORGE LOW

"Give me a millionaire with a fast backswing and I can have a very enjoyable afternoon.

—George Low

George Low may not have been "born retired," as Jimmy Demaret once said, but he has elevated hanging around golf tournaments to an art form.

In fact, he was born not far from the Baltusrol Golf Club in New Jersey, where his father was head professional. If young George was in awe of Baltusrol's prominent membership, he didn't let on. One of his tricks was to solder a dime to the shop floor and watch the assorted millionaires embarrass themselves trying to pick it up. On another occasion he asked a member who had just taken a handful of free tees if he was "planning to start a bonfire."

George, who was a fine player, came to the public's attention after Arnold Palmer credited him with some advice that turned his putting around. This led, however briefly, to George having a full-time job with an equipment company. He soon saw the error of his ways and went back to doing what he's done better than anyone else in the game's history—hanging around.

*M*any years ago George found himself in a match with the Duke of Windsor and one Robert R. Young, a railroad tycoon, at Seminole.

Despite all the golf he played, the duke wasn't much of a threat on the course, and George won easily. As they strolled to the clubhouse, George kept waiting for the duke to reach into the royal pockets and cover his losses. The duke never made a move, and George, being the impatient type, began to nervously clear his throat. Finally Young took George aside and discreetly explained the realities of life among royals.

"George, perhaps I should have mentioned this sooner, but the duke never pays off his wagers," he said.

"He don't what?" George asked, stunned that he had just wasted a good four hours on a stiff.

"His Royal Highness feels that it's rather an honor to play in his company and, therefore, he shouldn't consider paying," said Young.

"Mr. Young," said George, "from now on, you take care of your railroads and I'll take care of my dukes."

DAVE MARR

*A*BC Sports golf analyst Dave Marr is one of the truly great hang-around guys in golf, which, coming from a writer, is about as high praise as there is. One of the pleasures of the game is spending time with guys like Dave, listening to stories about the places and players they've seen over the years. Dan Jenkins once said that what set Dave apart was that he was the only player he'd ever seen who actually picked up a check.

Herbert Warren Wind, the elegant writer for *The New Yorker* in reflecting upon Dave's win in the 1965 PGA Championship, delicately observed that for a long time he feared that Dave was just too intelligent to win a major championship. Herb's point was that Dave's range of interests and curiosity precluded the sort of tunnel vision that golf at the highest levels seems so often to require.

Be that as it may, there's no doubting that those same qualities make him one of the truly special people in the game.

*G*oing into the final round of a tournament, especially a major, your mind does funny things," says Marr. "You want to concentrate on the job at hand, but all these thoughts keep entering your mind. The morning of the last round of the PGA, I got a note from my cousin, Jackie Burke. It read, 'Fairways and greens, Cuz.' That simple little thought suddenly brought everything into focus."

●

I was paired once with Jerry Barber, who could be— how do I say this?—very strong willed. He snap-hooked one of the ugliest drives you'll ever see and immediately glared at me and said, 'You started walking,' like it was my fault. I wasn't in the mood for listening to Jerry's act, so I said, 'Yes, Jerry, I put one foot in front of the other, and the next thing you know I'm walking,' which is just what I did."

●

*W*hen I was—I don't know—thirteen or fourteen, I went off to play in the Texas Junior, which at that time had all kinds of really good players. After the qualifying round, I saw that I was supposed to meet Don January in the first match of the second flight. He was like a god back then, so I walked up to him, introduced myself, and told him I really looked forward to playing him the next day.

" 'Forget it, pipsqueak,' he said. 'I don't play in the second flight of anything.' "

MERION GOLF CLUB

*T*he 11th hole at Merion Golf Club outside Philadelphia is one of the most celebrated and historic—not to mention difficult—holes in golf. It is where Bob Jones closed out Eugene Homans, 8 and 7, in the finals of the 1930 U.S. Amateur, Jones's last major championship.

Everyone in golf has his or her own opinion about which are the great courses, the great players, and so on. I have a theory about great holes. A great hole is one that, by virtue of either design, history, or sheer beauty, can literally give you goose bumps. The 12th at Augusta is one, as is the 17th at St. Andrews, the 17th at The Country Club, or the 16th at Cypress Point. When you stand on the tee of the 11th at Merion and read the plaque commemorating Bob Jones's win, goose bumps the size of gutta-perchas rise up and remind you that you are in the presence of greatness.

●

*F*our years after Jones's win, Bobby Cruickshank came to this hole leading the 1934 U.S. Open by two shots in the final round. The 11th is a short par 4, and Cruickshank needed just a 9-iron for his approach. He hit a weak shot and was certain that the ball would wind up in the brook that guards the green. To his utter surprise, the ball bounded off a rock in the brook, landed on the green, and pitched up toward the hole.

Cruickshank, stunned but delighted, said, "Thanks be to God," tossed his club high into the air, and walked toward the hole, forgetting all about the club—at least until the club thudded into his head, slashing open a deep wound. The wound did him in, and Olin Dutra went on to win the Open. Cruickshank, who had survived a German POW camp in World War I, finished third.

●

*T*he Bobby Cruickshank story, like a few others in this book, highlights just how intense, and occasionally humiliating, golf can be, particularly at the highest levels.

Bob Toski, the wonderful player and teacher, once offered this analysis of the game:

"Some people try to argue that golf isn't really a sport, because there's no physical risk. But they're wrong. Physically golf is a nonviolent, noncontact sport, but all the violence is inside you. Look at Bob Jones. He'd lose tremendous amounts of weight in the course of a championship. At the end of a round his necktie would be so knotted with sweat that he'd have to cut it away. Byron Nelson couldn't keep food down prior to a round. That's what makes a player like Nicklaus, who thrives on pressure, so remarkable. The champions in this game are the players who can control the violence inside themselves."

*I*n 1971 the actor Yul Brynner came to Philadelphia for a production of *The King and I*. He had his agent contact a local real estate agent and arrange for a "lovely, big house in a quiet area where I may have some peace and quiet during the day."

The broker knew just the right house, a rambling old affair bordering Merion in the exclusive suburb of Ardmore. Brynner came by, inspected the property, and, declaring it ideal, moved in on Sunday.

On Monday the U.S. Open moved in across the street.

DR. CARY MIDDLECOFF

*D*oc Middlecoff might just be one of the most under-rated players in the game as well as one of its best storytellers—a wonderful combination to have in a friend if you happen to be a writer. Despite a relatively short (fifteen-year) playing career, he won thirty-eight tournaments, including two U.S. Opens and a Masters. He's seventh on the career win list. One of the pleasures of the game is spending a few hours in the evening with him, listening to his stories about the game and the people who play it.

●

*W*hen I won the 1949 Open at Medinah I really didn't play that well, but I made every putt I looked at," he says. "Coming down the stretch, I was worried about Sam [Snead] and Clayton Heafner. I finished ahead of them, and all I could do was wait. Sam needed pars on 17 and 18 to tie but bogeyed 17. Clayton had an eight-footer on the last hole to tie, but he missed it. After his round, a USGA official, trying to console Clayton, said, 'You should have won this one.' Clayton, who was just mad all the time, threw a drink in the guy's face.

"In 1957 I was defending my Open title at Inverness

and had a twisting, downhill ten-footer on the final hole to tie Dick Mayer," Doc recalls. "People make a lot of the fact that I was a deliberate player, but I'm like Jack [Nicklaus]. I just can't bring myself to pull the trigger until I'm ready. The longer I looked at this putt, the more impossible it seemed. I just couldn't get a line. Finally a guy in the gallery yelled out, 'Hit the damned thing!' I looked up, startled, really, and said, 'Listen, fella, you can yell all you want, but as long as I don't hit this putt I'm still the Open Champion.' Maybe that calmed me down, because I made the putt. Of course, Dick went on to win the playoff, but I was real proud of that putt."

●

*L*ike every good golfer, Doc occasionally succumbed to the pressure of competition and the sheer difficulty and innate unfairness of the game. The most celebrated case came in the 1953 U.S. Open at Oakmont in Pittsburgh.

"I just hated late starting times," he remembers. "I hated the waiting around and the spiked-up greens. At Oakmont I let that begin to eat at me. I played all right on the front side, but on 10 I hit my second shot into a bunker. Well, that just did it. I was never a good bunker player in the first place, and this just put me over the edge. I looked over there at the Pennsylvania Turnpike, which cuts through the course, and I said to myself, 'I don't have to take this any more.' With that, I just slashed the ball out of the bunker and sent it running down the turnpike. I motioned to my caddie and started in. One of the players asked me if it was in my pocket. 'No, my ball is on its way to Ohio, and I may just play Inverness tomorrow.' "

THE NATIONAL GOLF LINKS

*T*he National Golf Links in Southhampton was
founded by Charles Blair MacDonald, a very wealthy
and autocratic golf enthusiast, who patterned many of the
holes after some of the more famous holes in Scotland.

MacDonald had a wonderful approach to members who
had complaints or suggestions about the club. If he
thought the ideas had merit, he would commission the
job—billing the member for the work. In one case he
overheard a member grumbling about the vast swarms of
mosquitos rising from a pond on the 14th hole. MacDonald ordered the pond drained and billed the startled member, who was advised to either pay up or leave.

MacDonald's nephew, Peter Grace, announced rather
boldly, after playing the course with his uncle for the first
time, that it was simply too easy. For example, he said,
the first green could be driven with a good shot.

"Don't be ridiculous, Peter," C. B. shot back. "No one
has ever come close to reaching the green. Nonsense."

With that, the two headed for the first tee, where Grace
hit what could arguably have been the most expensive
shot in golf history. His drive rocketed off the clubface,
bore through the prevailing wind, bounced, and rolled
onto the front edge of the green. His uncle, horrified,
marched away without uttering a word. He didn't need to.
That night he wrote his impetuous nephew out of his
will—a decision that cost Peter Grace $1 million.

BYRON NELSON

"The man was just awesome. When I had to play him I'd say, 'Oh, dear Lord, please get this over quick. There's just no stopping him.'"
—George Fazio, on facing Byron Nelson

*T*ry to figure the odds on Sam Snead, Ben Hogan, and Byron Nelson being born in the same year. Or Nelson and Hogan coming out of the same caddie yard.

Of the three, Nelson enjoyed his success earliest and retired soonest. Some say he quit because he had nothing left to prove. Others suggest his nerves finally became frayed. For his part, Nelson says he and his late wife, Louise, simply tired of the travel. He had won enough money to buy and run a comfortable ranch near Dallas, which is what he set out to do in the first place.

●

*P*eople will always debate who was the greatest player in history. But when you ask who best personified the term "gentleman," Byron's name is always at the top of the list.

"When I was still an amateur, Byron and I played a

111

series of exhibitions around California," recalls Ken Venturi, who, like Tom Watson, was a protégé of Nelson. "I learned a lot during that time. After we played he'd go over my round, asking me why I played a certain shot or hit a certain club. He was trying to refine my playing. But one thing I'll always remember from those exhibitions is that when we arrived at a course Byron would quietly find out what was the course record and who held it. If it was held by the local pro or amateur, he'd never try to break it. He knew that record meant more to them than it would to him. That's a perfect example of the kind of man he is."

●

*W*hen Byron Nelson first came east from Texas early in his career, he found a job as an assistant pro at Ridgewood, a fine club in New Jersey. One day a member asked Byron, who even then was noted for his uncanny accuracy, if he thought he could hit a flagpole off in the distance. Nelson took a 1-iron and hit the flagpole on the first try, presumably to the astonishment of everyone but himself.

●

*B*yron Nelson would rank high on anyone's list of the best ball-strikers, but on at least one occasion he was too accurate for his own good.

"By 1957, I had been off the tour for quite a number of years, but I decided to play in the Masters and was having a pretty good tournament. I was paired with Peter Thomson in the final round and came to the 16th hole at even par," Byron explains. "My tee shot was right on line but it spun back off the green and into the water. I moved to the front of the tee and changed clubs, hitting a 7-iron. The ball went into the cup on the fly, bounced out, spun back through the bunker and into the water. I took another drop, got the ball on the green, and took two putts for a seven. Do you know the ovation I got when I walked off the green was as loud as any I ever got for winning a tournament?"

●

Golf history records Nelson's incredible year in 1945 as proof, along with his wins in the Majors, of just how great he truly was. In that year he won nineteen of the thirty tournaments he entered, including eleven in a row. His average was a remarkable 68.33 strokes per round. But consider what he did in one tournament—just one stretch in a tournament—when he played what he admits was the best golf of his career.

The tournament was the 1942 Masters, when he faced Ben Hogan in a playoff and edged him, 69-70. Nelson was three strokes behind after six holes. He birdied the 6th, eagled the 8th, birdied the 11th, 12th, and 13th, and played the next three holes in even par. Hogan played the same stretch in one under par and lost five shots . . . and the Masters.

WILLIE NELSON

*I*f you had to pick an unlikely person to be an avid, totally off-the-wall golf addict, it probably wouldn't be Willie Nelson, with his ponytail, jeans, and T-shirts. But the truth is that he's gone so far as to build his very own course back home in Austin, Texas.

"It's my own damn course, and I can do anything I feel like out there," he explains. "I can wear what I want. Drink what I want. Play with who I want and not play with who I don't want to play with. Par is whatever I say it is. I've got one hole that's a par 23, and yesterday I damn near birdied the sucker."

JACK NEWTON

*A*ustralia's Jack Newton was a player of enormous potential whose career ended tragically one evening when he walked into the propeller of a small plane, severing an arm. Still, in his brief time onstage he turned in remarkable performances, most notably in the 1975 British Open at Carnoustie, where he lost to Tom Watson by a shot in a playoff, and in the 1980 Masters, where he finished second to Seve Ballesteros.

Like so many international players, he toughened his game on the foreign circuits. Some tours were tougher than others, as this story about an African tournament, Cock o' the North, reveals.

Newton was playing the 17th hole at the Ndola, and as he studied his third shot he heard his caddie shriek, "Ants, Bwana!" as he dropped the bag and raced away.

Newton stood transfixed until hundreds of ferocious African ants began to tear at his body. Newton began to slap at his body frantically but to no avail, since the beasts are virtually indestructible. Finally he began ripping away his clothes, right down to and particularly including his undershorts, where the ants had begun to swarm with a special frenzy.

Stark naked and assisted by his wife, who did what little she could to shield him from the gallery, he managed to rid himself of the ants and, somehow, finished his round.

But, as they say, everything that goes around comes around, and the next day Newton spotted a particularly attractive woman standing alongside one of the fairways. As Newton, as was his wont, studied the woman, she suddenly began slapping at herself wildly. Newton knew what was coming next, and as surely as night follows day soon she was totally exposed to the bright African sun.

As unlikely as it seems, given all the distractions, Newton went on to win the tournament.

JACK NICKLAUS

"He plays a game with which I'm not familiar."
—Bob Jones, after watching Jack Nicklaus win the 1965
Masters

*I*t's easy to get into an argument about who is the greatest golfer of all time. As Sam Snead once said, "I don't know who was better, Joe Louis or Muhammad Ali. All I know is, I wouldn't want to be in the ring with either of them. All you can try to be is the best of your time."

Jack Nicklaus is easily that. He's won more Major championships than any other player, and only Snead has won more tournaments or played as well for as long.

I have two images of Jack Nicklaus that will last a long time.

The first came in 1986 at the Masters. I was working in Butler cabin with Tom Weiskopf and Brent Musburger. On Sunday Jack hit his tee shot to 16 stiff for a birdie. When the camera picked up the ball and it looked as though it might go in the hole, Weiskopf was electrified in a way that I had never seen in the years he'd worked at CBS.

"He's going to do it," said Weiskopf, in awe. "He is going to win it again."

Later, when it was clear Jack had won, he was brought

to the cabin. Hundreds of people waited outside, chanting, "Jack, Jack, Jack!"

A year later he and his wife, Barbara, were at Jupiter Hills watching their son Gary try to qualify for the match-play rounds of the U.S. Amateur.

With nine holes remaining, Gary gambled on a reachable par 5, only to miss the green to the right. His first attempt to recover failed, as did the second, which produced a flash of anger from the teenager.

At that point, the man many feel is the greatest player in history quietly walked ahead to the next hole, alone with his thoughts.

●

*I*f I had to pick one story about Jack that best describes him it would be one that goes back to the British Open in 1977 at Turnberry," recalls Nicklaus's friend Ken Bowden, a former editorial director for *Golf Digest*. "Prior to the last round we had made plans to have dinner. That final round, when Tom Watson beat Jack by a shot and they both played such phenomenal golf, was breathtaking, but it was a very emotional loss for those of us who are close to Jack. It was the only time I can remember Barbara in tears. I sought Jack out following his interviews and told him that I'd completely understand if he wished to cancel dinner.

"He put his hand on my shoulder, looked me right in the eye, and said, 'What's the matter, Kenny? It's only a game.' It hit me right then that that's who Jack Nicklaus really is."

I've always said that Jack is the greatest player in history," says Lee Trevino. "But I've also said that if he had to play my tee balls he'd be back in Columbus running the family drugstores.

"One year we were paired together at the Tournament of Champions. I hit my drive on the first hole into the fairway, and Jack hit his into the rough. I said something about hitting the fairways at La Costa, and Jack said if he hit the ball as far as I did he could keep it in the fairways, because he'd be hitting 5-irons all day. When he finished his round, I'd shot around par and Jack had come in with just a terrible score, way over par.

"As we walked off the course, I said, 'Jack, I know what you should have done today.'

" 'What's that?' he asked.

" 'You should have hit your 5-iron,' I said, and he just laughed and shook his head."

•

*I*n the 1969 Ryder Cup matches at Royal Birkdale, Nicklaus faced Tony Jacklin in the final match of the competition. They came to the last green tied—the outcome of the match was on the line.

Nicklaus putted first, sinking a treacherous putt to assure a tie. Then in one of the greatest examples of sportsmanship in his long career, he conceded Jacklin's two-and-a-half-footer.

"I knew you could make it," he said, as he walked off the green with his arm over Jacklin's shoulders. "But under the circumstances, I wasn't about to make you try."

*A*rnold Palmer is ten years older than Jack Nicklaus. When Nicklaus joined the PGA Tour in 1962 he had already won two U.S. Amateur championships, and many people were wondering what would happen the first time Nicklaus went head-to-head with Palmer, then the best and most popular player in the game.

As luck would have it, the site of their first major duel would be the U.S. Open at Oakmont Country Club in Pittsburgh. This was Palmer's backyard. He was the hometown boy who made good, and at the end of 72 holes Nicklaus and Palmer were tied, forcing an 18-hole playoff.

"I can beat the fat kid on his best day," Palmer confided to a friend on the eve of the playoff.

It wasn't to be. Nicklaus went out the next day and won, 71-73, for his first tour win and his first of four U.S. Open titles.

●

I've always enjoyed caddying for Dad, and, of course, I'm in awe of him as a player, but I saw a side of him at the Memorial Tournament that I'll never forget," recalls Jackie Nicklaus, the oldest Nicklaus child. "We came up to 18, and Dad was out of the tournament. Since the Memorial is in Dad's hometown [Columbus, Ohio] the gallery was standing and going crazy. You couldn't hear yourself think. It was the most deafening roar you can imagine. I couldn't believe it. I got all choked up, and tears started running down my face. I was a little embarrassed about that until I looked over and saw Dad crying too.

" 'Son,' he said, 'this is what it's all about.' "

*T*he pressures of tournament golf are enormous; perhaps more than any other player, Jack Nicklaus seemed to thrive upon them. But that's not to say that he handles all types of pressure equally as well.

He was in the hospital for the births of all five of his children and fainted four times out of five.

"Jack," said one doctor after yet another Nicklaus swoon. "The baby is fine, and Barbara is fine. In fact, you had a longer recovery period than she did."

GREG NORMAN

*B*y now the litany of catastrophes that have befallen
Greg Norman on a golf course is the stuff of legend.
Bob Tway got him from a bunker on the 72nd hole of the
1986 PGA. Larry Mize followed up by chipping in on the
2nd hole of a playoff for the 1987 Masters, and on and on
it goes. But perhaps this streak of incredible misfortune
got its start back at the 1982 European Open at Sunningdale.

Norman was leading the tournament going into the 7th
hole in the final round. The hole requires a drive that
rises sharply in order to clear a rise of land just off the
tee. Ordinarily this would not present a problem for Norman, one of the finest drivers in the game.

Norman teed his ball, stared into the distance at his
target, squared his massive shoulders, and took the club
back steadily from the ball, coiling powerfully and totally
at the top of his backswing—a textbook position to de-
liver a fearsome rip into the ball. But it was just at this
split second that an earthworm poked its head through
the ground a mere inch or so behind Norman's ball. One
can only imagine what raced through Norman's brain at
this point. There is nothing in golf or life that can ade-
quately prepare you for such a shock to the system.

Norman reacted instinctively, minutely altering his swing to miss the offending worm. Of course, at the same time he barely made contact with the top half of the ball, sending a low screamer into the bank, where it plugged deep in the heather, gorse and what have you.

It should come as no surprise that the 1982 European Open was not won by Greg Norman.

MOE NORMAN

"What am I going to do with another toaster? I've already won twenty-seven of them."
—Moe Norman, explaining why he tanked the last few holes of a tournament so he could win a radio (that he had already agreed to sell) instead of a toaster.

*I*f you've never heard of Moe Norman, you're not alone. He may be the best player Canada has ever produced. He certainly is the most—how should we say this?— unique. People rank him with the Hogans of the game for his ball-striking ability. Why didn't he win more tournaments? Read on. . . .

●

*P*laying in a tournament in Canada, Moe was told that all he had to do was part the final hole to set a course record.

"What is the hole?" he asked, and was told it was just a driver and a 9-iron. With that, he hit his 9-iron from the tee, followed it with a driver off the fairway, then sank the putt for a birdie and a course record.

In another tournament he came to the final green with a three-shot lead. Just to make things interesting, he chipped his ball off the green and into a bunker, and then got up and down for the win.

●

One year he was invited to play in the Masters. Apparently the history and tradition of the event didn't have much of an effect on Moe.

As he stood on the first tee in the first round, he decided to fire his caddie. So after hitting his drive, he set off down the fairway carrying his own bag. Before he could reach the green, Clifford Roberts came racing out in a golf cart, bringing a new caddie and hoping to placate the fiery Norman. Roberts succeeded, at least until the next day when Moe walked off the course in mid-round, claiming it was too windy for golf, and took a bus home to Canada.

●

Moe was persuaded, however briefly, to play the American Tour. The problem was that he was in such awe of some of the players that he spent much of his time summoning the nerve to ask for autographs. Still, he did have his moments in the sun.

In the Los Angeles Open he hit his opening drive from atop a bottle of Coca-Cola. He hit another drive from atop a tee marker, then, for good measure, had his caddie roll a ball to him and hit a 250-yard drive while the ball was still moving.

*A*ll good golfers seem to have outstanding eye-hand coordination, and that is certainly true of Moe Norman. Once, while waiting on a tee during a tournament, he began to idly bounce the ball off the face of his driver. A spectator bet him $1 per bounce over and under one hundred bounces. Moe was still going strong at 184 bounces when he deliberately stopped and collected his $84 from the ashen-faced man.

"I could have gone all afternoon, but I didn't want to hold up the tournament," he explained.

CHRISTY O'CONNOR

*I*reland's Christy O'Connor, referred to reverentially by his countrymen simply as "Himself," was one of the purest players in the game's history. He was a member of ten Ryder Cup teams, winning almost forty percent of his singles matches and might have won more if he hadn't been so naturally caught up in the fellowship of such affairs—a temptation he faced in the 1963 World Cup matches at St. Nom la Bretèche near Paris.

Moments before he was due to tee off, he sat in the locker room nursing a hangover of unbearable proportions and pleading with a writer from a London paper to bring him some coffee. The writer begged off, pointing out to O'Connor how unseemly it would be to have Ireland's greatest champion stagger to the first tee armed with a jug of coffee.

"Fine, then," said O'Connor. "Get some coffee. Some very black coffee. Go down the first fairway to the 200-yards stake. From there, march off sixty-five paces and wait in the woods for me."

"Yes," said the writer.

"With very black coffee and lots of the stuff," reminded O'Connor, not losing sight of the important details.

The writer, loaded with a steaming mug of the elixir, waited patiently deep in the woods. He heard the crack of the ball off O'Connor's drive and the telltale rustle of the ball crashing to earth through the canopy of leaves. He saw the ball land, very nearly at his feet, followed soon after by O'Connor, who had just hit one of the greatest tee shots of our time under unspeakable pressure.

MAC O'GRADY

"There's a little boy in all of us. The trick is knowing how to let that child come out."

—Mac O'Grady

*M*ac O'Grady is as enigmatic a guy as ever played the tour. I first met him when I was taping a feature for CBS called "Flakes on Tour," and Mac certainly qualified for the piece. He could play almost as well left-handed as right-handed and once inquired whether he could play in the U.S. Amateur as a lefty.

Mac endured seventeen attempts at the tour's qualifying school before getting his card. Once he made the tour he won twice, but sadly, most of his energies seemed consumed in a running battle with Commissioner Deane Beman and his staff. In the end—at least at this writing—Mac has left the tour to work on his research on the golf swing and other elements of the game and, perhaps to find what has eluded him so far—happiness and peace of mind.

*A*fter a year or so on tour Mac came to me and asked what he was doing wrong," recalls his friend Gary McCord. "I told him that he was trying too hard, that he had to just let things happen. I told him he had to somehow learn patience.

"Well, damn if Mac didn't head over to Palm Springs and spend the day driving around behind elderly people. He figured that following people who were going fifteen miles an hour was a pretty good way to learn patience. I don't know if it worked, but it damn near got him arrested a couple times when the old folks got nervous and called the cops."

THOMAS P. "TIP" O'NEILL

*B*ack in the first years of the Reagan administration, I convinced *Golf Digest* that we should do a piece on Tip O'Neill. Through mutual friends at the *Boston Globe*, I reached one of the Speaker's assistants, Chris Matthews, and he set up the phone interview. The interview, which was supposed to run for ten minutes, lasted nearly an hour and traced his love affair with the game from his boyhood in Cambridge, where he caddied for Bob Jones, then a graduate student at Harvard, and through his political career.

At the time, the Republicans had singled out the Speaker as a symbol of what was wrong with the Democratic party and the country. He was getting bashed pretty hard—and unfairly—by Reagan's lackies. That being the case, I was delighted when Chris Matthews called and said that the Speaker had laughed more during our interview than he'd laughed in a long time.

I saw the Speaker a few years later, just after his retirement. At that time he mentioned that he'd had a course in Cambridge named in his honor. I asked him if it was a public course.

"Public? My God, you can get starting times in six different languages," he laughed.

Beautiful.

I started out as a caddie, and I'll tell you, I almost got fired right off the bat. I'm caddying for this fella, and it's in the fall. Well, he hits his drive off into the woods, so I hung his bag up in a tree and began looking for the ball. Well, it was a brown leather bag, and by the time we found his ball I had lost the bag. Christ, we looked all over the place but didn't have any luck. You can imagine the guy was a little hot under the collar, but I promised I'd make it up to him. Sure enough, a few weeks later, once the leaves had fallen, I went back out with my pals and found it, but it was a close call. I thought I was going to be working for him for the rest of my life."

●

O ne day I'm playing with Sammy Snead and a couple guys down at Pine Tree in Florida. Now the most I ever play for is a few bucks, but we get into it, and I wind up losing a hundred or so, all fair and square, mind you. Off we go to the clubhouse for a pop and a little gin rummy. Now I'm a pretty good gin player. As a matter of fact, I'm one of the best. I got my hundred back plus a little extra.

"As Sammy gets up to leave he shakes my hand and says, 'O'Brien, you're a hell of a fella. What 'ya say you do for a living?' "

●

I 'm playing in the Hope one year with Lee Trevino. We get to this water hole, and I pull out an old ball and toss it down on the ground.

"What are you doing?" says Trevino. "Put down a new ball and show me a practice swing."

So I figure what the hell, the guy's a pro, I'll give it a shot. I put down the new ball and take a swing.

"Hold on," says Trevino. "Put the old ball back down."

FRANCIS OUIMET

When the 1913 U.S. Open came to The Country Club in Brookline, Massachusetts, a young amateur from the neighborhood, Francis Ouimet, was in the field. To be sure, nobody gave the twenty-year-old former caddie much of a chance, but when Ouimet beat the great English professionals Harry Vardon and Ted Ray in a playoff, it put golf on the map in this country.

As with the case of so many champions, golf was indeed fortunate to have in Ouimet a fine player who was a genuinely decent human being. Witness this story from that fateful day he won the Open.

●

Anyone who assumed that the Open win would change Ouimet was reassured by an encounter he had with an older member of The Country Club just after the awards ceremony.

"Well, Francis, I suppose this means you'll be too busy to play with any of us now," he said.

"No sir," Ouimet replied. "What are you doing Tuesday afternoon?"

ARNOLD PALMER

*F*ew players have captured the public's affection or admiration the way Arnold Palmer did in the late 1950s and the 1960s. He was "Arnie," and they loved him and his bold, attacking style. And perhaps more than any other player, he reciprocated their affection with his generosity. Theirs has been a thirty-year affair of the heart.

No public figure has ever suffered fools as gladly as Palmer. He has infinite patience. Indeed, he seems to derive strength from his galleries. The recent trend that's seen some athletes and other celebrities selling their autographs absolutely horrifies Palmer, who may have signed more of them than any man on earth.

"Anyone who would charge for an autograph ought to be ashamed of themselves," he says. "It's an honor and a privilege to be asked for an autograph. I just don't know what's wrong with these people."

●

*T*he Wilson Sporting Goods Company asked me to go to the 1954 U.S. Amateur to take a look at this kid from Pennsylvania named Palmer," recalls Gene Sarazen. "He won it, but I never thought he'd amount to a hill of

beans. He hit the ball all over the lot but made enough putts from all over the place to win the championship. Still, I told Wilson to forget it. Shows you how much I know."

•

A rnold called me one day when I was working at the *Pittsburgh Press*," recalls Bob Drum. "He said he's got a guy who wanted to pay him two thousand bucks to write a golf book. He says we'll split it fifty-fifty. Well, Christ, I'm making $60 a week at the paper, so this was like dying and going to heaven.

"I asked him when we could get together, and he said that was the problem. The guy wanted the book in three months, and Arnold was going to be gone. I asked him what the hell I was supposed to do. I didn't know anything about golf. I was a baseball player. He says to me, 'All you have to know is two things: take the club away slow and hit it hard.'

"Well, I couldn't very well write a book with just that, so I went to the Pittsburgh Public Library and got out every book I could find on golf. I stole a chapter from each book, and that's how Arnold's first book got done. The only question was what we should call it: *Take It Away Slow* or *Hit It Hard*. We called it *Hit It Hard* 'cause *Take It Away Slow* sounded like a porno book.

"A few months after the book came out, I decided I should learn how to play this golf. I called Arnold and told him I wanted to come up to Latrobe and get a lesson from him. He said, 'You don't need to come up here. Everything I know is in the book, just read it.'

" 'Read it!' I yelled at him. 'I wrote the damned thing!' "

*A*rnold Palmer traveled to St. Andrews for the 1960 British Open. On the first day he came to the historic Road Hole, the 17th, a dangerous par 4. "What should I hit?" he asked Tip Anderson, his caddie.

"Five-iron," he replied. Arnold disagreed but hit the 5-iron onto the green, then three-putted for a bogey.

The same thing happened in the second and third rounds, and when they reached the fairway on 17 in the last round, he was very much in contention with Kel Nagle. He and Tip again argued over the club selection. Tip wanted him to again hit a 5-iron. Arnold wanted to hit the 6. He finally did hit the 6 and put it onto the road, but he managed to get up and down for his only par on the hole that week.

"See, Tip," Arnold joked as they walked to the final tee. "You gave me the wrong club all week, and it cost us the championship."

●

*P*rior to the 1990 British Open at St. Andrews, Palmer announced that, barring any unforeseen circumstances, it would be his final British Open. At age sixty, he felt it was time to move off center stage.

Palmer played valiantly, getting from the galleries the thunderous applause and loving adulation that he, as much as anyone in the game's history, so deserved. It appeared certain that he would make the cut.

But golf is not always fair—or dramatic. When the scoring was finished on Friday, he had missed the cut by a single shot.

That evening Palmer was in the Jigger Inn with his longtime caddie Tip Anderson and some friends. Anderson was inconsolable.

"I should have done better," he said, as tears streamed down his weathered face.

"No," said Arnold, taking Tip's hand in both of his. "We should have done better, old friend."

●

*P*almer was paired with Dave Marr in the final round of the 1964 Masters. He had a comfortable lead over Marr and Jack Nicklaus as he came to the home hole. The galleries were huge and loud, cheering their great hero home. Palmer, conscious that Marr was dueling Nicklaus for second place, asked his friend if there was anything he could do to help.

"Sure, Arnold, you could take a 12," quipped Marr.

●

*A*rnold had more patience for people than anyone I ever met," recalls Dave Marr. "The thing about him is that he really likes people, which I think he got from his father, Deacon, who was a club pro in Latrobe. I mean, you'd really have to work at it to get Arnold mad, but a guy did one night in P. J. Clarke's.

"Arnold and Winnie (his wife) were having dinner with Frank Gifford and his wife, and there was a guy at the table behind them who kept trying to goad Arnold. He knew Arnold had to leave the next day to go overseas, and so he kept at him, saying that there wasn't any difference between the pros and a good amateur—I believe the guy was a pretty good local player—and that he'd take Arnold on any local course for a $500 nassau if Arnold would give him one a side.

"Arnold was very patient about the whole thing and told the guy that as much as he'd like to play, he had to leave the next day. Well, the guy starts up with his friends like he had just backed down the great Arnold Palmer. With that, Arnold whirled in his chair and said, 'Listen, I'll play you tomorrow morning at Winged Foot. Only I'll give you two a side and we'll play a $5,000 nassau. Are we on?' Frank said you could hear the guy gulp from across the room. He just looked down at the table and didn't say another word."

●

*I*f Palmer has been good with the galleries, he's been uncommonly patient with the press, which is in some ways even more impressive when you consider how many times he's been asked the same—often dumb—questions.

In the 1961 Los Angeles Open, he came into the pressroom and was asked how he managed to make a 13 on one hole.

"It was easy," he said. "I missed a twenty-footer for a 12."

HARVEY PENICK

"Mr. Penick is the most balanced person I have ever known or expect to know. I never heard him say an unkind word about anyone. Just knowing him has been a life lesson for all of us."

—Ben Crenshaw

"Thinking must be the hardest thing we do in golf, because we do so little of it."

—Harvey Penick

*H*arvey Penick is easily one of the most beloved and respected teaching professionals in America. He started caddying at the Austin (Texas) Country Club in 1913 as an eight-year-old. Ten years later he was named the club's professional.

Since that time the club has changed locations three times ("I might be the only pro to ever wear out three courses," he laughs softly), but he has remained a fixture. In addition to his work at Austin Country Club he coached the University of Texas team for thirty-two years.

Perhaps unfairly, like any teacher Harvey Penick is best known for his pupils—and what pupils they are—Ben Crenshaw, Tom Kite, 1975 U.S. Women's Open Champion

143

Sandra Palmer, Kathy Whitworth, and the late Maurice Williams, just to name a few. Typically, however, his greatest pride comes from the help he's given hundreds, maybe thousands, of average players.

"I've been privileged to work with players like Ben and Tommy," he says. "But it's no feather in my cap that they became good players. They would have been good players without me. For a teacher to take someone who can't get the ball airborne and help them so they can enjoy the game—now that's something to be proud of."

●

I was in a terrible slump and went to Mr. Penick for some help," recalls Ben Crenshaw. "He watched me hit four or five balls, then stopped me. He came over, put his hand on my shoulder, and said, 'Don't you ever wait this long again to come back and see me.' He didn't raise his voice, but I believe he was as mad as he'd ever been. We worked hard and got me squared away. Before I left he gave me a wonderful piece of advice. He said, 'Ben, just remember that it takes just as long to play your way out of a slump as it did to play your way into one.'"

"Mr. Penick used to charge $5 an hour for his lessons, and people were always after him to raise his fees. He always argued, 'I use small words, so how can I charge big prices?' Finally the board ordered him to raise his fees. He did it, but he was never very happy about it."

—Tom Kite

"You have to make corrections in your game a little bit at a time. It's like taking your medicine. A few aspirin will

144

probably cure what ails you, but the whole bottle might just kill you."

—Harvey Penick

"I think almost all players would be better off learning one good shot and then making adjustments for the wind. It's just a whole lot safer to play the shot you have confidence in. [Former University of Texas football coach] Darrell Royal told me he'd never call a play in a game that his team hadn't already practiced. That's a pretty good rule for golf, too."

—Harvey Penick

"There are two things the players on the tours should realize: adults will copy your swing, and young people will follow your example."

—Harvey Penick

●

*T*ommy Armour once paid me a wonderful compliment. He told Betty MacKinnon that he was only the second-best teacher in the game. He said I was the best. But you can't let things like that go to your head. I came back from a seminar once and said to my wife, Helen, 'Imagine, fifty of the game's greatest teachers all in one room.'

" 'Harvey,' she said, 'there was one less great teacher there than you think.' "

"A pretty girl will always have the toughest time learning to play golf, because every man wants to give her lessons."

—Harvey Penick

"I don't wish to sound pretentious in any way, but I've always tried to teach by using stories or parables. I figure if it's good enough for the Bible it's good enough for Harvey Penick."

—Harvey Penick

PINE VALLEY GOLF CLUB

Whenever people are asked to select the best course in the United States, Pine Valley in Clementon, New Jersey, invariably winds up near the top, if not at the top, of the list. It is a beautiful yet fearsome test of golf that inspires both awe and terror for golfers of all skill levels.

In the 1920s a fine British player, Eustace Storey, came to the punishing 2nd hole, paused, and said to his host: "I say, do you chaps actually try to play this hole or do you simply photograph it and go on?" he asked.

●

The opening stretch of holes at Pine Valley is as demanding as any in golf. Much to his own amazement, J. Wood Platt, a gifted amateur in the 1920s, found himself four under through four. As he reached the tee on the 226-yard, par 3 5th hole he simply headed for the adjacent clubhouse.

"I'm going in, gentlemen," he said to his playing companions. "It's got to go downhill from here, and I'm going to quit while I'm ahead."

●

*B*ritish writer Bernard Darwin played the first seven holes in level par, hit a good drive on the short 8th hole, then took a 16. He retired to the clubhouse and announced, "It's all very well to punish a bad stroke, but the right of eternal punishment should be reserved for a higher tribunal than a greens committee."

●

*P*ine Valley deserves a place in golf history, if for no other reason than the role it played in Arnold Palmer's marriage to Winnie.

Just out of the Coast Guard with only a fine amateur reputation to his name, he wanted to marry Winnie but didn't have enough money for even a modest engagement ring.

Some friends told Palmer they'd pay him $100 for every stroke under par 72 at Pine Valley, but he had to pay $100 for every stroke over 80. Palmer toured the course in 68, bought the ring, and lived happily ever after.

147

GARY PLAYER

*F*ew players came as far and accomplished as much as South Africa's Gary Player. He is just the fourth player, joining Jack Nicklaus, Ben Hogan, and Gene Sarazen, to win all four of the modern professional majors, and he has won all but the U.S. Open more than once.

Player is a True Believer. In his heart of hearts he believes that nothing is impossible, and in the final analysis that attitude may wind up being his greatest legacy to the game, for when a generation of young players around the world—people like Seve Ballesteros, David Frost, Greg Norman, and Nick Price—saw Player beat the best American players, they realized they could do it as well, and professional golf became a truly international game.

●

*P*layer began his international playing career in 1955, when he left South Africa for the Egyptian Match Play Championship, which he won. The victory inspired him to set out for England, where he found himself in position to win a minor event in Huddersfield.

Coming to the last hole, he believed he needed a 4 to win. Desperate, he chose a driver but hooked the ball wildly. It came to rest near a stone wall. Player had two choices: he could take an unplayable lie and virtually ensure second place, or he could try to bounce the ball off the wall and, hopefully, ricochet the ball onto the green. He carefully studied the wall, determining just the proper spot to drive the ball. Satisfied that he had the shot properly planned, he hit the ball as hard as he dared, only to have it bounce off the wall, hit him squarely on the chin, and knock him out.

Still, being merely knocked cold was not enough of an obstacle to stop Gary Player. He recovered enough to pitch the ball onto the green and make the putt for what he believed was the win.

Wrong. His playing companion had the sad task of telling the distraught Player that not only had he knocked himself out but he had also incurred a two-stroke penalty for hitting himself with the ball. And if all that weren't enough, he later learned he could have won the tournament with a 5 on the last hole.

•

*G*ary greatly admired Ben Hogan, and Ben, I think, saw a lot of himself in Gary," says Gardner Dickinson. "I believe they had discussed having Gary play Hogan clubs, but he got an offer from Dunlop and went with them. I don't think he realized how Ben felt about that decision. Anyway, he called Ben one night from South America and asked if he could ask some questions about his swing.

" 'Gary,' Ben said, 'I'm going to be very curt with you. What kind of clubs are you playing?'

" 'Dunlop,' said Gary.

" 'Well,' Ben said. 'Call Mr. Dunlop.' "

*F*or all his wins in the major championships, it might well be that the most revealing round of his career came in a semifinal match against Tony Lema in the World Match Play Championship in Wentworth, a 36-hole affair which found Player seven down after the morning round.

A lesser person might well have ceded the afternoon match to the fates and gone into the tank, but not the Player. As he lunched in the clubhouse, he couldn't get from his mind the image of the gallery deserting his match for the other semifinal. Nor could he bear the humiliation he was certain to feel by losing so badly in such an important competition.

Such thoughts drove Player's game to a higher level. Suddenly he felt energized and resolved to prove everyone who considered his plight hopeless to be quite wrong.

Player cut Lema's lead to five on the front 9, picked up another hole with a par on the 10th, then lashed a tremendous drive on the 11th to set up a birdie and another win. Lema's lead had been cut to a manageable three, and the tide had turned decisively in Player's favor.

On the 13th, as demanding a driving hole as there is in the game, Player's drive cut the middle of the fairway, while Lema's ball hooked into the woods. He bumped the ball back into play, but his third shot ended up well short of the hole. Player's approach set him up for a possible birdie. Lema's hopes rested on his making the long, par-saving putt and the chance that Player would miss his ten-footer for birdie. Lema made his. Player did as well.

Two down, five to play.

The next two holes were halved. On the narrow 16th Player risked a driver, and the gamble paid off magnificently. Lema, struggling from the tee, chose a 3-wood. Again he hooked his drive and, again Player won the hole.

Now one down with two holes remaining, Player watched as Lema holed his putt. Now, unless Player followed suit for a half, the match—and his remarkable comeback—would be ended. As he had all afternoon, Player pulled off the crucial shot. The putt fell. The match went to 18, a par 5.

Lema's second shot came up short of the green, while Player, struggling to reach the green in two, pushed his approach into the trees down the right side. After a few anxious moments, he heard the roar from the grandstand as the ball kicked out of danger and ran up toward the hole. Lema's pitch was short. Player evened the match, then went on to win on the first extra hole, completing one of the greatest comebacks—and collapses—in golf history.

●

Gary Player's mother died when he was quite young, and much of the responsibility for raising Gary fell to his older brother, Ian, whom he adored. One day the boys were out for a five-mile run when Gary tired and fell to his knees, saying he couldn't go on.

" 'What do you mean, you can't finish?' Ian raged, pulling me to my feet and cuffing me firmly. 'You can do anything you set your mind to do. There's no such thing in this world as *can't*. You must eliminate the *t*. With that, he pushed me forward and would not allow me the luxury of stopping. That is how I learned to persevere."

*L*ike many people in all walks of life, Gary Player draws strength from adversity. If he feels he has something to prove, or that people are not for him, he kicks his game up an added notch. That was the case in the 1978 Masters, when he staged a valiant comeback on the back nine. At first, his assault drew little attention from the galleries, which was just the boost he needed.

"Gary, he is a great fighter," recalls his playing companion that day, Seve Ballesteros. "He said, 'Seve, these people don't think I can win. I will show them, wait and see.' "

He birdied seven of the last ten holes to tie the course record 64 and win his third Masters.

BOB ROSBURG

*A*nyone hanging around San Francisco when Bob Rosburg was a teenager might have picked up the clues
that Rossie had, as they say, a feel for the game.

For starters, as a fifteen-year-old he clocked the legendary Ty Cobb, 7 and 6, in the Club championship at the
Olympic Club. The members teased Cobb so mercilessly
that he quit the club and never came back. Rossie went on
to win the 1959 PGA and finish second in the U.S. Open
in 1959 and 1969. He had a reputation for one of the best
short games in history, as well as for being outspoken—
a quality he's brought to his work as a commentator on
ABC's golf coverage.

●

*R*ossie was playing a practice round in Memphis when
a rules official came by in a cart. Rossie asked him if
he was going to mark off an eroded area as ground under
repair. The official told him that he wouldn't because it
wouldn't come into play during the tournament.

Of course, the next day Rossie came to the hole in the
first round and found his ball lying on the bare ground. At
that point he called for a rules official. When the official
arrived, he looked at the ball and then looked at Rossie.

"You didn't have to bring me out here, Rossie," he said. "You know I'm not going to give you a drop."

"I know that," said Rossie. "I just wanted a ride in. I'm picking up."

●

*L*ike so many players of his era, Rossie played by sight, not yardage. And he played fast. In one tournament he was paired with a young player who consulted his yardage book on every shot—and took a long time doing it.

On the first hole he hit his approach over the green. On the next hole he left it short. The worse he played, the more he dawdled and toiled over his yardage. Finally Rossie had seen enough.

"Boy, if you didn't have that yardage book you'd be in a hell of a mess, wouldn't you?" he said.

THE ROYAL AND ANCIENT
GOLF CLUB OF ST. ANDREWS

*P*rospective captains of the R & A are required to "drive themselves in" by hitting a tee shot off the first tee at the Old Course during the club's fall meeting. Some meet with more success than others.

In 1922 the Prince of Wales fortified himself for the task with a few stiff pops at the Grand Hotel's bar. He weaved his way through the mist, arriving at the tee where Andrew Kirkaldy, the honorary professional, prepared to tee his ball.

"This is an awful job," said the prince.

"Just keep your eye on the ball, sir," said Kirkaldy.

If he did, he saw the most famous heel job in history, as the ball squirted sharply to the left, where it came to rest in the Valley of Sin fronting the 18th green.

"My God, if he holes it we've got a new course record," cried a member of the gallery.

THE RULES

"What a stupid I am."
—Roberto de Vicenzo, after learning he had lost the
1968 Masters after signing an incorrect scorecard.

*T*he rules of golf are many and complicated. Over the
years, untold rules-related disasters have made the
news. The most prominent was, of course, the de Vicenzo
incident.

De Vicenzo, an affable and popular Argentinean, began
the final round of the 1968 Masters by chipping in on the
first hole. Since it was his forty-fifth birthday, the gallery
broke into "Happy Birthday." He responded with birdies
on the next two holes and turned the front side in 31. He
finished with a bogey on 18 for a 65, signed his scorecard, and waited to see how Bob Goalby, his closest
pursuer, would finish.

As de Vicenzo was being interviewed, his playing companion, Tommy Aaron, realized to his horror that he had
incorrectly given de Vicenzo a 4 instead of a birdie 3 on
17, and a total of 31-35-66. Since a player is responsible
for the score he signs for, de Vicenzo, instead of tying
Goalby and facing a playoff, had finished second.

Behind the scenes, Bob Jones and Clifford Roberts pored over the rules hoping against hope to find a ruling that would absolve de Vicenzo. No chance.

In the end, nobody really won. De Vicenzo garnered worldwide sympathy, but all that ultimately mattered was that he had blown a Major. Goalby, a fair and decent man, had a stigma attached to his greatest win through no fault of his own.

●

*P*eople don't realize this, but a fella offered Bob and Roberto a chance to play a winner-take-all match for a lot of money, $100,000, I think," says Sam Snead. "I told Bobby he should play. What the hell, he was as good a player as there was in the game at that time. But I think Clifford Roberts got wind of it and killed the idea."

●

*J*ackie Pung, a fine player from Hawaii, had a similar experience at the 1957 U.S. Women's Open at Winged Foot.

Pung finished at 298, but when officials checked her card they noticed that her marker had given her a 5 on the 4th hole instead of the 6 she made. While her total was accurate, they had no choice but disqualification.

While it was small consolation for the title she lost, the members at Winged Foot promptly raised $3,000 for Pung—$1,200 more than the first prize won by Betsy Rawls.

*A*ustralian Kel Nagle, who won the 1960 British Open at St. Andrews, was another victim of the scorer's pencil.

Playing in the 1969 Alcan Golfer of the Year Tournament in Portland, Oregon, he opened with 70 and was in contention in the second round until officials discovered that his marker had entered his first round total, 35, in the space for his score on the 9th hole. Nagle technically had a smashing 105 for his day's labor and went from being near the lead to earning a lock on last place.

●

A similar fate awaited Miller Barber and his partner, the outstanding amateur Harvie Ward, at Spyglass Hill one year during the Crosby. Barber shot a 68 on his own ball, and with Ward's help they had a team score of 62. Sad to say, they marked their score for the back 9 in the box for the 18th hole. Instead of leading the tournament, they posted a staggering 101.

"It was a tragedy," said Miller. "That's all you can say."

●

*T*ommy Nakajima came to the par 5 13th in the 1978 Masters and, gambling on his drive, put it in the creek on the left. He took a drop and a one-stroke penalty, then laid up short of the green. His approach backed into the water fronting the green, but the ball was playable. Almost. It failed to clear the hazard, rolled back, and hit him on the foot. Two more penalty strokes. Then, to top it off, his caddie dropped a club in the hazard for two additional strokes.

The wonder is that he finished the hole at all.

*M*ental meltdowns with a scorecard are certainly not the only heartbreakers when it comes to the rules. There's the matter of starting times, which officials take very seriously.

Gary Player found himself stuck in traffic en route to the 1990 World Series of Golf. For a person of Player's tenacity, a little thing like a few hundred cars jammed up is a mere trifle. Player simply looked around, spotted a Hell's Angels–type biker, and talked him into ferrying Player through the crowd.

●

*S*eve Ballesteros, then twenty-three, should have kept a bit better track of time at the 1980 U.S. Open at Baltusrol. Then the reigning Masters and British Open Champion, Seve was a favorite to win his first U.S. Open title. He missed it by roughly seven minutes, which is just how late he was for his starting time and just how long it took him to leave the club and head for the airport.

●

*O*f course, rules being rules, it's also a bad idea to get started too early, as six players found out at the 1940 U.S. Open at Canterbury.

Johnny Bulla, Porky Oliver, Dutch Harrison, Ky Laffoon, Duke Gibson, and Claude Harmon were finishing lunch when they noticed storm clouds building on the horizon. Figuring they'd get out ahead of the storm, the group divided into threesomes, headed for the course, and teed off twenty-eight minutes ahead of their starting times.

The resulting disqualifications were costly for each player but especially painful for Oliver, whose final round 71 brought him in at 287—tied with the eventual champion, Lawson Little.

●

*C*addies are wonderful people to have on your side. They cheer you up when you're down. They come up with all kinds of useful advice. They can be an enormous help in a tournament—except when they aren't.

Probably nobody was ever hurt more by a caddie than Byron Nelson in the 1946 U.S. Open. His caddie accidentally kicked his ball on the 16th green during the third round. For his caddie's clumsiness, Nelson earned a penalty stroke.

The caddie was shattered and in tears, but Nelson, true to character, put his arm over the boy's shoulder and said, "It's all right, son. I was a caddie once myself, and it could have happened to me."

Nelson finished the championship at 284, in a tie with Lloyd Mangrum, who won the 36-hole playoff the following day.

Then there's the tale of Leonard Thompson, who faced a long, twisting eagle putt in the 1978 Quad Cities Open. Thompson put a good stroke on the ball, and as it approached the hole his caddie began gyrating wildly, which was all very well and good until a tee fell from behind his ear. Thompson's ball struck the tee. Thompson's scorecard recorded a two-stroke penalty. Thompson's caddie did not record a big tip for his efforts.

*W*hile the rules are, strictly speaking, the rules, they are subject to interpretation. One such case concerned South Africa's Bobby Locke at the 1957 British Open at St. Andrews.

Locke, who had already won three British Opens, came to the final green with a three-shot lead and his ball just two feet from the cup. As a courtesy to his fellow player, he marked his ball a clubhead's length from its resting place. But in all the excitement, Locke failed to replace it in its original position when it was his turn to putt. Technically he could have been disqualified for signing an incorrect scorecard, but the championship committee showed that the quality of mercy is occasionally alive and well. They waived any possible penalty and let his winning score stand.

For his part an appreciative Locke, in a gesture of gratitude, allowed that he would forever swear off his trademark plus-fours, which he had worn throughout his golfing career—although what one had to do with the other remains a mystery.

GENE SARAZEN

*O*nly four men have ever won each of the four modern
Major championships—the Masters, the U.S. and
British Opens, and the PGA Championship—and Gene
Sarazen was the first to do it, leading the way for Ben
Hogan, Gary Player, and Jack Nicklaus. By winning seven
majors, Sarazen easily ranks as one of the game's true
legends. Ironically, he is best known for making a double-
eagle 2 on the par 5 15th in the last round of the 1935
Masters—a shot that helped put the tournament on the
sporting map of America.

●

I had been in good shape after two rounds, but I shot a
73 in the third round, and that gave Craig Wood a
three-shot lead," Sarazen recalled one day as he sat outside the clubhouse during the Masters. "Craig had finished, and I needed birdies on three of the last four holes
to catch him. I was paired with Hagen, who was on his
way to a 79, and he kept telling me to hurry up because
he had a date that night. We came to 15, and I hit a good
drive but still had a long carry over the water. My caddie
talked me into taking a 4-wood and giving it a chance. It
was at about that point that Bob Jones came down to

watch Walter and me finish. And he was about the only one there at that point. The writers were all sitting around the clubhouse drinking. They had already filed their stories with Craig as the winner.

"I took the 4-wood and toed it in a little. I was pretty sure I could reach the green, but I wasn't sure I could keep the ball from running through the green. I hit it perfectly. I knew it would be close, and a few seconds later what few people there were in the gallery let out a roar.

"There was a boy on a walkie-talkie back to the club-house. He kept shouting, 'Mr. Gene done made a two! Mr. Gene done made a two!' But everyone thought he meant I made a birdie on 16. A few minutes later, when people figured out what had happened, this crowd began storming down into the valley. I parred in and then won the playoff the next day, 144–149.

"It's a funny thing. Over the years I've met thousands of people who claim they saw me hit that shot, which is impossible. It always meant a lot to me because both Jones and Hagen saw it. Years later, whenever I'd go over to Asia, I'd always be introduced as 'Mr. Double Eagle.' If people didn't know I was a golfer, they'd have thought I was an Indian chief."

S arazen's great friend and sternest rival was Walter Hagen, who was, among other things, a master of gamesmanship.

In one tournament Hagen and Sarazen were paired in the final round, and it was clear matters had come down to a head-to-head match between the two men.

Prior to his round, Sarazen received a package containing an orange necktie and a note that read, "Dear Gene: I'm sure you won't remember me but I'm the blond from the Follies. Please wear this necktie for good luck. I will be in the gallery but don't look for me."

Sarazen went out and played a sloppy front side, his concentration divided between his golf and his search for the mysterious blond. By the turn, he was trailing Hagen and his good-luck tie, soaked by rain, had begun to run all over his shirt.

"Kid, where'd you get the beautiful tie?" asked Hagen.

"From a friend," snapped Sarazen.

"Just a friend?" asked Hagen, who could no longer contain himself and broke out laughing. Hagen won the match easily.

BOB SHEARER

*T*he value of an understanding and supportive wife cannot be overstated, but in some cases logic and common sense override even the strongest wifely devotion.

Consider the case of Kathy Shearer, wife of Australian professional Bob Shearer, who called the clubhouse during the 1980 Atlanta Classic and asked what her husband shot.

"63," came the reply. "No, Shearer. S-H-E-A-R-E-R," she replied.

SHELL'S WONDERFUL
WORLD OF GOLF

"I don't even like golf, really. I just like watching the show because I get to see places I've never been."
—Red Smith, on the old Shell series.

S hell's Wonderful World of Golf" was a delightful series that ran through much of the 1960s. It featured the best players from around the world, playing on many of the greatest courses in the game. It had segments on local color. It had instruction. It had Jimmy Demaret and Gene Sarazen. There's no telling how many thousands of people took up the game as a result of this series. Even today tapes of some of the matches, such as Snead vs. Hogan at Houston Country Club, are collector's items.

*W*hen we first started we really didn't know very much about golf, especially the crew," remembers Fred Raphael, who produced and directed the series and later created the Legends of Golf Tournament. "Our first match was at Pine Valley. We were under a tight deadline because the club's president, John Arthur Brown, would only let us shoot on Sunday after four. Byron Nelson was playing Gene Littler. Byron hit an absolutely perfect drive on the first hole. I looked up in horror as one of the crew picked up the ball and ran back to the tee.

" 'Could you hit it again, Mr. Nelson,' he said. 'We missed it.' "

●

*W*hen we first started the series we couldn't pay by check, so we'd arrive at a location and Shell would get as much cash as we needed," recalled Jimmy Demaret. "We were in Portugal for one show, and they sent us an accountant with a briefcase filled with $25,000 in cash. We were driving to the course, and we ran into a police roadblock. Somebody had robbed a bank, and they were checking every car coming out of the city. I figured we were goners, but they never checked our car. They never checked the robbers' car either, so I guess the fix was in."

I was playing a match at Sunningdale, and when I was clearing customs in London this clerk asked me if I was there for business or pleasure," recalls Dave Marr. "When I told him I was there for the Shell show he asked for my work permit, which I didn't have, and proceeded to put a very formal British tap dance on my head. I got a little hot, and pretty soon the guy announced he was sending me back to the States on the first plane. Fortunately, cooler heads prevailed, and they agreed to let me stay overnight. The Shell people pulled some strings, and the next morning I went back to the airport to get checked through. Wouldn't you know it, the same clerk was on duty. As he stamped my papers he said, 'Perhaps if you'd been somebody more famous, say Hogan or Palmer, there wouldn't have been such a problem.' "

●

I stopped by a bar near my office one day, and one of the matches was on," remembers Fred Raphael. "I said to the bartender, 'I bet you so-and-so wins.' He asked me how I knew, and I told him I'd produced the show. Every week he'd ask me who won. I thought he was just being friendly. It turns out he was making a fortune betting on the shows."

WALKER B. SMITH

*F*ew people have ever even heard of Walter B. Smith, but in his own way this turn-of-the century figure stands as testimony to the spirit—and spirits—of the game.

Smith was a member at the exclusive Tuxedo Park Golf Club just north of New York City. One day he stood on the first tee and announced, "Golf requires two things: courage and the ability to keep your eye on the ball."

"This supplies the courage," he said, producing a silver flask of scotch and taking a deep swallow. He then produced one of his spare glass eyes (he had lost an eye as a child) and laid it down near the ball. "And now I keep my eye on the ball." With that, he swung mightily and sent the ball rocketing down the fairway.

SAM SNEAD

"I never saw Byron Nelson play, and I've only seen Ben Hogan hit balls, but I've played a lot with Sam, and he plays the game the way it's supposed to be played—the way you dream about playing just once in your life."
—Ben Crenshaw

"Like the classic plays and symphonies, Sam Snead doesn't belong to just one generation. His mark will be left on golf for an eternity."
—Peter Thomson

*F*or every person who's imagined he or she has played with Arnold Palmer's fearless abandon or has won championships with Jack Nicklaus's grace and courage, there are hundreds who, in their mind's eye, believe they possess a swing as pure and powerful as Sam Snead's. Of course, none of them do. No one else ever has.

It's an interesting but impossible exercise to name the best golfer of all time, but here's something worth trying: Tom Weiskopf rates players by ranking them from one to ten with every club in the bag. It's not a bad approach, and if you ask people who have been around the game at the highest levels, they'll put Sam at or damned near the

top in every category. When I rank Sam this way, it comes out something like this:

- Driver: Nine. Nobody was ever longer, especially into the wind. The trade-off you face with length is accuracy, and occasionally the sheer power of his swing would result in a hard hook.
- Fairway woods: Ten.
- 1-iron: Ten. It was as though the club was created just for him. He could hit it long and straight and work it at his will. Maybe the best ever.
- Long irons: Ten. Same as with the 1-iron, even more so.
- Middle and short irons: Ten. Unsurpassed, mostly because he has such great feel and could do so many things with his clubs. Where most people fall back on one kind of shot under pressure, it was impossible to hide a pin from Sam.
- Pitching wedge: Ten. Try him sometime. While most people automatically reach for a sand wedge for short approaches, Sam was a virtuoso with the club that was, after all, designed for them.
- Sand wedge: Ten. Only Gary Player ever came close.
- Putter: Nine. Uncanny with long approach putts, not quite as good with shorter putts, but nobody wins what he won without being a great putter.

There are two things I've always wondered about when it came to Sam. First, how many more tournaments would he have won if he played today and didn't have to hold down a club job or do as many outings and exhibitions as he did? Second, how many U.S. Opens would he have won if he could have gotten one under his belt early?

In the end, nobody can tell. But when I think of Sam, I always come back to a conversation with Dave Marr.

"Of all the players I've seen, I'd say Rossie [Bob Rosburg] was the most natural," said Dave.

"What about Sam?" I asked.

"Sam doesn't count," Dave replied. "Sam is supernatural."

●

S am had played in the 1937 British Open, finishing eleventh, but didn't enjoy the experience. The travel was tiring and expensive, and playing in the cold winds was not a challenge he chose to face again anytime soon. Still, when World War II ended, there was pressure on him to play at St. Andrews when the Open resumed in 1946. Not the least of that pressure came from Wilson Sporting Goods, with whom Sam had a lucrative endorsement contract. Still, until virtually the last minute Sam hedged on making the trip. Finally, in desperation, his manager, Fred Corcoran, enlisted Walter Hagen to help convince Sam to make the trip.

"What's his problem?" Hagen asked Corcoran as they waited for Snead to finish his round in a tournament.

"He says he can't putt," Corcoran replied.

"He always says that," Hagen said. "Leave him to me."

When Sam came into the clubhouse, Hagen took him to the far end of the locker room. He told him that the large double greens at St. Andrews were perfect for Sam's game and then asked him to stroke a few putts.

"Raise your blade a little at address, Sam, and then try to slap the ball just above the equator," said Hagen. "All you want to do is get the ball rolling with topspin. You do that, and you'll win that Open, Sam."

Sam looked at Hagen as though he were crazy. He'd never heard of doing anything as bizarre as deliberately topping putts. Then he looked at ball after ball rolling as though they'd been hit by a machine and decided that maybe Hagen wasn't so crazy after all.

As luck would have it, the following day one of the New York papers ran a headline, "Hagen Gives Snead Putting Lesson—Picks Slammer to Win British Open." Fine, except right next to the story ran Sam's syndicated instruction column, headlined "How to Putt, by Sam Snead."

●

So Sam traveled to St. Andrews for the 1946 British Open. As the train pulled into St. Andrews station, he looked out his window across the Old Course, the most venerated course in the game.

"Look yonder at that farm there," he said to his traveling companion, Lawson Little, pointing to the course. "It looks like that might have been an old golf course that's gone to seed."

Not surprisingly, his comments found their way to the British press, which had a field day at Sam's expense.

Sam went on to win, and when the ceremonies finished, his caddie, Scotty, approached, begging him for the ball he won with.

"Mr. Snead, if you could find your way to part with that ball I should treasure it all my life," he said.

"I gave him the ball, and he went right down the street to the nearest pub and sold it to the highest bidder for fifty quid," Sam recalls. "He made more money than I did that week."

*S*am was playing a practice round at Augusta National with Tom Kite and young Bobby Cole from South Africa, who was playing in his first Masters. Sam hit a fine drive on the 13th, the dogleg left par 5. As Cole prepared to play his shot, Sam said, "You know, junior, when I was your age we'd drive the ball right over the corner of those trees."

Cole hit a towering drive that crashed two-thirds of the way up into the pines.

"Of course, Bobby, when I was your age, those trees were a hell of a lot smaller," Sam said, as he walked off the tee smiling.

●

*T*hroughout much of his career, Sam—and his manager, Fred Corcoran—got a lot of publicity out of the fact that Sam was raised in the Virginia mountains.

Corcoran was fond of telling the story about the time Sam won a tournament in Los Angeles and Fred showed him a copy of the *New York Times* with his photo on the sports page.

"Hell, Fred, how'd those boys get my picture?" Sam supposedly asked. "I've never even been to New York."

●

I pretty much enjoyed playing in big-money matches, but some of them were a little scary," Sam remembers. "Once, about 1938, Mr. Icely, the head of Wilson, called me and said he wanted me to go to Cuba to play in a match for a friend of his. It seemed the guy had a big bet with a Cuban millionaire named Sanchez. Sanchez was willing to bet a ton that nobody could beat his club pro, Rufino Gonzales, on his home course. I didn't want to go, but Mr. Icely insisted, so off I went.

"I got down there to Cuba and played a practice round with Rufino. I shot a 65, and while he was a good driver and a great putter, I knew I could handle him because I could reach the par 5s and he couldn't.

"The next day we played, and when I got to the first tee I noticed all these real mean-looking thugs. Somebody pulled me aside and explained that Batista, the dictator, had bet heavily on Rufino in the match and these were his boys out to make sure there was no funny business. On top of that, there were so many bets down that the pot was over $100,000. I was in there for $250, but that was the least of my worries.

"I won the match with 69-68 to Rufino's pair of 71s, but when we were walking to the clubhouse I was sweating bullets because Batista's boys were closing in around us. I got my winnings and hightailed it back to Florida, where Mr. Icely asked how I'd done.

" 'Just fine, Mr. Icely,' I said. 'But if it's all the same to you, next time you get a match like that set up, send Jimmy Demaret. He likes to travel, and he'd make a prettier corpse than I would.' "

●

*O*ne day I'm out fishing, and, because it's so hot, I'm wearing a baseball cap instead of my straw hat," says Sam, beginning a story that shows his ability to laugh at himself. "I see this old-timer looking me up and down, trying to figure out who I am. Finally he comes up and says, 'Excuse me, you're somebody famous aren't you?'

" 'Well, I believe you might have heard of me,' I replied.

" 'You're a golfer, right?' he said.

" 'That's right,' I said.

" 'I knew it,' he said, all excited. 'You're Ben Hogan!'

"He ruined my whole damn day."

*F*or many years *Golf Digest* held its Senior Tour event, The Commemorative, at Newport Country Club in Rhode Island. One year Sam and Chandler Harper agreed to a nassau with Bob Goalby and Dow Finsterwald during a practice round. Harper had complained about a sore back, and on the first tee Sam had to help him tie his shoes.

"Now look here, fellas," said Sam. "Chandler's in bad shape. He needs a little weight. Give him a couple a side to make it fair, and we can have a game."

Goalby and Finsterwald happily agreed. Sam made seven birdies. Chandler made six. They won easily.

"You cheating SOB," said Goalby good-naturedly to Sam.

"Cheating?" Sam protested. "How was I supposed to know Chandler was going to make such a great comeback?"

●

*S*am was playing in a tournament on the day of the 1948 presidential election. When the early returns began to come in, Fred Corcoran told Sam, "Dewey's leading."

"What'd he go out in?" Sam asked.

●

*A*nother time Sam was in the clubhouse when Corcoran came in and announced, "Bing Crosby won the Oscar."

"Is that match or medal?" Sam asked.

*Y*ou know, Jimmy Demaret started this story about me burying my money in tomato cans out in my backyard," says Sam. "I never thought anyone would take it seriously until my wife called me at The Homestead one night and said there was some guy out digging up the backyard."

●

I used to play a lot of so-called goodwill exhibitions with Demaret. One time we're off in some country or another, and I'm getting ready to play from a bunker, and I heard Jimmy say, 'Sambo, look behind you.'

"Well, Jesus, if there isn't this huge ostrich fixin' to take a bite out of my hat. I put up my arm, and she must have thought I was gonna hit her, 'cause she latched onto my hand. It was two weeks before I could play again."

●

I came out on tour in '37, and I didn't know many of the fellas," Sam said. "I arrived at one stop and was looking for someone to play a little practice round with. I ran into Dutch Harrison and Bob Hamilton and asked if I could join them. They said sure and asked if I wanted a little wager. I wasn't much on gambling, but I wanted to get along, so I agreed.

"Well, I hit my first two drives out into the boonies, and I just knew those boys were wondering what they got themselves into. Hell, I wasn't too sure myself, but pretty soon I settled down and began matching them shot for shot.

"After a while I was getting the better of them, and old Dutch tried to give me the needle about my so-called strong grip.

" 'Young man, you've got a fine swing there,' Dutch said. 'That terrible hook grip doesn't seem to bother you a lick.'

"I'd heard that before, so I just ignored him and tried a bit harder. By the end of the day, I'd won a little money from those boys and told them I sure would like to play again the next day.

" 'Sonny,' said Dutch, 'you work your side of the street and we'll work ours.' "

●

*O*ne reason I've been able to play so long is that I've kept my hand in it," Sam once explained. "If I had taken two weeks off without touching a club it would have taken me a month to get my game back, which is what most so-called weekend players don't understand. They think golf's a game you can just lay down and pick up like a favorite rifle. I went on a safari to Africa one time. To keep my swing in shape I used to play the other guys for a little money. We didn't have any balls, so we'd play with animal droppings. I had the edge though. When my brothers and I were kids we'd hit horse droppings because what balls we could find we'd sell over at The Homestead. The trick is to hit them on the dried-out side. I knew that, but the other guys didn't, so theirs would keep breaking. They never did figure it out."

ST. ANDREWS

*"It is a wonderful experience to go about a town where
people wave at you from doorways and windows, where
strangers smile and greet you by name, and where simple
and direct courtesy is the outstanding characteristic."*
                                    —Bob Jones, on St. Andrews

St. Andrews is said to be the birthplace of golf, but it
is more than that. It is the repository of the game's
soul as well.

Consider just some of the players who have won the
British Open on the Old Course: J. H. Taylor, James
Braid, Bobby Jones, Sam Snead, Peter Thomson, Bobby
Locke, Kel Nagle, Bob Charles, Tony Lema, Jack Nick-
laus, Seve Ballesteros, and Nick Faldo.

And then think for a minute about the old stone bridge
that crosses that Swilken Burn and realize that every
great player in the game's history—save Ben Hogan—has
walked upon it.

*F*or much of its history the Old Course was closed on Sundays. Once when Tom Morris, the professional, was approached by visitors and asked why, he replied, "You may not feel the need to rest on the Sabbath, but the Old Course does."

In 1958 Bob Jones traveled to St. Andrews as captain of the American team to compete in the first world Amateur Team Championship for the Eisenhower Cup. On this trip he received the Freedom of the City, an honor he shares with just one other American, Benjamin Franklin.

Jones, crippled with the spinal ailment that led to his death in 1971, spoke to the hushed audience for some ten minutes. He closed his emotionally wrenching acceptance by noting, "I could take out of my life everything except my experiences at St. Andrews and still have a rich, full life."

Unable to walk, he left the stage in an electric cart. As he made his way down the center aisle, the hall echoed with a tearful rendition of the old Scottish song "Will Ye No' Come Back Again?"

Sadly, he never could.

●

*F*or the people of St. Andrews, golf is a birthright. It is a passion almost universally shared. Their love for the game is deep and abiding, as is their reverence for those who have triumphed at its highest level. Witness this story about Bob Jones's return in 1936, six years after his retirement from competition.

After traveling to Berlin for the Olympics, he returned via Scotland, arriving unannounced at St. Andrews for a casual round on the course where he had won both the Open and Amateur championships.

Word of his visit raced through the town, and when he teed off following lunch, some two thousand townspeople had gathered to watch their beloved "Bobby."

"I shall never forget that round," he later wrote. "It was not anything like a serious golf match, but it was a wonderful experience. There was a sort of holiday mood in the crowd. It seemed, or at least they made it appear, that they were just glad to see me back, and however I chose to play was just fine with them, only they wanted to see it."

Jones would play the first nine in 32, but on the 8th tee he was paid what he would later call "the most sincere compliment I can ever remember."

As he put his club back in the bag, his young caddie looked up at him and said, "My, but you're a wonder, sir."

●

*T*here are a certain few holes known immediately to golfers around the world. The 12th and 13th at Augusta are two, as are the 16th at Cypress Point and the 18th at Pebble Beach. Throw in the odd 17th at the TPC at Sawgrass and you get the picture.

But the hole that heads the list is the dreaded 17th at the Old Course. The "Road Hole" is a 461-yard dogleg left par 4 that Ben Crenshaw calls "the greatest par 4 in the world because it's really a par 5." He's right in two ways. First, in the days of the hickory shafts and the featherie and guttie balls, it played as a par 5. But with the advent of modern equipment, it became a par 4 that has to be treated as a par 5 because of the havoc it can so readily inflict.

The trouble begins off the tee, as you face a blind drive over the corner of a building that used to serve as a railroad shed in the days when a rail line bordered the right side of the hole. A perfectly placed drive, then, must not only carry the building but flirt perilously close to the out-of-bounds stakes.

Had enough? But the fun's just begun. Depending on the wind, you then face a mid-to-long iron to a narrow, heavily contoured green guarded in front by a small but deep bunker on the left. Beyond the green lies the road, followed by a twelve-foot stretch of grass and then a stone wall. In other words, the target strongly suggests that the prudent golfer play short of the green, taking the trouble out of play, and then try to fashion a hellacious pitch somewhere near the hole for a par.

It is a testimonial to the hole's difficulty and historic ability to dispatch a player's championship dreams that during the Open the stands behind the hole are packed and the air thick with anticipation reminiscent of the Indy 500 when there's just enough moisture on the track to ensure calamity.

The Road Hole has claimed as its victims the famous and would-be famous.

Bob Jones came to the hole in the fourth round of the 1930 British Amateur. In those days the huge galleries were not kept behind the wall but were allowed to stand near the green. Tied with British Walker Cupper Cyril Tolley, whose approach was short of the green, Jones hit an attacking shot that carried over the green, striking an onlooker and rebounding to land ten feet from the hole.

Tolley, his nerves shaken by Jones's stroke of good fortune, made a brave pitch and sank the putt for par. Jones missed his birdie putt, and the match remained tied. Jones eventually won on the first hole of sudden death.

Good fortune continued to smile on America in the 1971 Walker Cup match when Vinny Giles, a former U.S. and British Amateur Champion, came to the 17th tied with Michael Bonallack, a five-time British Amateur Champion.

Giles hit his approach into the Road Bunker, while Bonallack left his approach safely short of the green, from where he pitched up to four feet. Giles's bunker shot ran over the green and onto the road. His next shot was hit thinly, getting only a few feet into the air. Incredibly, it struck the flagstick and dropped straight into the hole. Shaken, Bonallack missed his par putt, and Giles hung on to halve 18 and win his match.

Other notable catastrophes included Seve Ballesteros's drive out of bounds while leading the 1978 Open. The ensuing 7 effectively killed his chances, and he finished a disappointing seventeenth. But to prove that in golf what goes around comes around, Seve got a measure of revenge in the 1984 Open when Tom Watson, going for his third straight British Open title, came to 17 in the final round toe-to-toe with Ballesteros. Watson tried to fashion a high, soft 1-iron, but it got away from him, coming to rest virtually against the stone wall. Bogey was the best he could do, and his dream of a sixth British Open died on the Road Hole.

Perhaps the most infamous of all the crash-and-burns at 17 was the disaster suffered by Japan's popular Tommy Nakajima.

In the third round in 1978, Nakajima left his approach on the front-left part of the green, a position that forced him to hit his first putt dangerously close to the Road Bunker. His putt crested the hill, paused ever so slightly, then trickled into the bunker. He hit a delicate, spinning bunker shot that, again, got to the top of the ridge before returning to the sand. Sadly, it took him three more tries before he escaped the bunker. Two putts later, he had his 9 and the legend of the "Sands of Nakajima" was added to the lore of the Road Hole.

LEFTY STACKHOUSE

*L*efty Stackhouse had a temper. A considerable temper. As a matter of fact, as tempers go, he could have given the golfing world two or three a side and still been the best in history.

The stories about him are legendary. According to one, he missed a putt and, in the heat of the moment, hit himself in the head with his putter. The blow staggered him, sending him briefly to his knees, at which point he tried gamely to rise, only to collapse in a heap near the cup. Other stories are remarkably similar, except that they have Lefty punching himself in the head and knocking himself out. I tend to go with the latter. After all, who'd take a chance on ruining a perfectly good putter by smashing it against his head?

Other Lefty Stackhouse stories tell of the times when, after hitting a particularly grievous hook, he'd smash his right hand against a tree trunk or thrash it through a thorn bush, screaming obscenities at it as though it had a life of its own, independent of his brain and nervous system.

But the greatest of all the Lefty Stackhouse stories is the one that finds him playing in an exhibition tournament in Knoxville to sell war bonds. Everyone who finished the tournament would win something and on hand to present the awards and help attract the crowds was

Tennessee's greatest legend, World War I hero Sergeant Alvin York. York, a deeply religious man who disapproved of golf on the Sabbath (or anything else except church, for that matter), had a fanatical abhorrence of alcohol. It was pure fate, then, that he chose to follow a group that included Lefty Stackhouse, a man who approved mightily of both golf and distilled spirits on any day the combination presented itself.

Stackhouse, freed from the pressures of having to play well to earn a check, began drinking liberally from a bottle of Coca-Cola laced with alcohol. Soon the combination of his drinking and the heat began to take its toll. On one of the closing holes, he bent over to read the line of his putt—an unnecessary effort since, at this point, he could barely see the ball, let alone anything as sublime as the line. Spent by his efforts, he passed out and had to be carried to the clubhouse.

"That poor man exhausted himself," said a stunned York. "I had no idea this golf was such a strenuous game."

CURTIS STRANGE

*C*urtis Strange, who won the U.S. Open in 1988 and 1989, is arguably the most intense player on any tour today. After a fine amateur career he struggled early in his professional career, like most players. That struggle, plus his inherent candor and desire to succeed, has sometimes given people the wrong impression of Curtis. What some dismiss as temper, most of us who cover the game see as Curtis's singular pursuit of excellence. As a two-time U.S. Open Champion, no one ever strived to set a higher standard or better example—or tried more valiantly to make it three in a row.

•

*I*n 1976 I was the low amateur at the Masters and was brought into the press room for an interview," says Curtis Strange. "Usually they have one of the Yates brothers conduct the interview, but this time, for some reason, it was an older member, with white hair, a moustache, and an unbelievable southern accent. The reporters asked me a few questions but they really were more concerned with what was going on out on the course.

"There was a long pause and everyone thought we were done; then the member says, 'Curtis, I have a question.

You went to Wake Forest on an Arnold Palmer scholarship. How'd it feeeel to play with Arnold in the first round?' "

"Sir, I didn't play with Arnold in the first round," I told him.

"Oh," he said. "Well then, how'd it feel to play with the great Jack Nicklaus in the first round of the Masters tournament?"

"Well, sir, I didn't play with Jack in the first round," I explained.

"Well then, Curtis, just who did you play with in the first round of the Masters tournament?" he asked.

"Gay Brewer," I said.

There was a pause for a few seconds—maybe longer—then David Lamb, a reporter from Jacksonville, asked, mimicking the member's southern drawl, "Tell us, Curtis, how'd it feeeel to play with Gay Brewer?"

●

*P*laying in the 1980 Inverrary Classic, Curtis came to the last hole of the second round knowing he had to par the 445-yard, par 4 to make the cut.

As he and his caddie made their way across a narrow bridge to the tee, a spectator jarred the caddie, who lost his balance and his control of the bag. One by one the clubs began sliding out of the bag and into the deep water below. Splash, splash, splash went the woods. Splash, splash, splash went most of the irons. Finally Strange was able to grab onto the caddie, steady him, and take stock of the losses. There was a 2-iron, a 3-iron, a 5-iron, and a putter left. There was also a caddie, but given his recent performance, there was some doubt just how long he'd be around.

Now Curtis Strange is nothing if not a grinder. A solid

2-iron off the tee left him in 5-iron range. A good 5-iron left him with a two-putt par and a shot at the last two rounds. A local diver left him with a full set for the next day.

T. SUFFERN TAILER

*T*ommy Tailer was a figure out of F. Scott Fitzgerald. A man of considerable athletic skills that were complemented by his good looks, charm, and willingness to play for his own money, he was a legendary figure at the better clubs up and down the East Coast. Tailer did some of his best work at the exclusive clubs around New York where, in the 1930s, big money matches drew the better players from around the country.

●

I first met Tommy at a match that was arranged between us at Meadow Brook out on Long Island," remembers Sam Snead. "I'd just come out of Hot Springs, so not many people had heard of me. Tommy was one of the best amateurs in the area, so when these friends of his said they'd back me in a $500 nassau, Tommy was hot to trot. I lost the front 9 when he threw me a stymie on the 9th hole, but I won the back and the match.

"A year or so later I got a call from a guy named Bunny Bacon, another hot-shot New York amateur who liked to play for a little. He wanted me for a partner against Tommy and a Dr. Hochschield. The match was for $5,000, and I was guaranteed $300 plus expenses, win or lose, and an extra $300 if we won.

191

"By this time I was on tour and doing pretty well for myself, but when I showed up on the first tee, Tommy didn't seem too concerned. Before we teed off, Bunny laid off another $2,000 side bet with the doctor and then flashed me a look at the ten grand he was carrying. Now, I was used to tournament pressure and didn't mind playing for my own money, but seeing that $10,000 tightened me up a little. I topped my drive and my second shot, which brought Bunny a-runnin'.

" 'Sam, Tommy didn't get to you did, he?' he asked.

"I answered him with my clubs. While Bunny and the doctor slashed their way all over God's green acres, Tommy and I went at it right to the hilt. I had him dormie four, but he birdied 15 and 16. I finally eagled 17 to close him out, and Bunny wound up collecting $7,000.

"After we finished the match, we shook hands and Tommy said. 'Sam, I don't ever want to see you again.' "

●

*A*nother time Tommy got himself in a little financial stretch and had to take a Christmas job demonstrating a new board game where you'd roll a little marble along this board that had a bunch of holes in it," recalls Sam Snead. "It was hard to do, but Tommy had such good hand-eye coordination that he picked it up pretty quick, and he was quite a hit at the New York department stores where they sold them. Sure enough, he did so good that he built up a little stake for himself and headed south for the winter. Right off the bat, he got hustled by a couple guys down at Indian Creek in Miami for all of $2,000.

"Tommy didn't have much of a temper, but I heard he was hot when he got back to the locker room. Lo and behold, what did he spot but one of these games he'd been selling. He knew he was home free.

" 'My, my, what's this?' he asked, and before you knew it, he had those boys on the line. He tanked the first couple of tries, just to build up the pot, then ran the tables both forward and back, nicking those boys for all he'd lost plus a little extra."

TITANIC THOMPSON

*I*t would be inaccurate, and also unfair, to dismiss Alvin Clarence "Titanic" Thompson, who died in 1974, as simply a hustler or gambler. He was a keen student of both the odds and human nature, and he used that knowledge to his best advantage. He was a fine player who realized early on that the disparity between tournament purses and the money he could easily lift from the unsuspecting was too great to pass up.

"Titanic asked me once if he thought he could beat anyone playing left-handed if he got nine-and-a-half shots a round," remembers Paul Runyan. "I told him I thought that was quite possible. He went to Dallas and played several rounds in the 80s to set the trap. He then offered to play left-handed with strokes. He won $5,500 the first day and naturally said it would only be sporting to give the boys another chance. They bit, and he wound up winning over $20,000. That night he was leaving a casino, and a caddie tried to rob him. He shot him with the .45 he always carried, killing him instantly. I should add that it wasn't a lucky shot. Ti was an extraordinary shot."

*O*n one occasion—and probably more than once, actually—Thompson bet people that he could throw a peanut over a tall building, such as a warehouse. Now throwing anything that small and that light that far is extraordinarily difficult, unless the object is loaded with lead, as Ti's peanut was. He won the bet easily.

●

*O*ne time Ti bet a guy a lot of money that he could shoot a bird out of the sky with his .45," recalls Sam Snead. "Now Ti was a hell of a shot, but that's damned near impossible . . . unless you've got birdshot, which Ti did."

●

*O*nce, when he was in Illinois for a tournament, Thompson met a farmer driving down a road with a truckload of watermelons. He stopped, counted the melons, and bought the entire load on the spot. The only stipulation was that the farmer had to drive past a hotel in town where Ti knew there would be gamblers staying. At the appointed hour, as the farmer came down the road, Thompson bet the gamblers that he could guess the exact number of watermelons. They bet, he gave them the number, and he made a small fortune.

LEE TREVINO

*L*ee Trevino came from terrible poverty to become one of the finest players in history. Along the way he became incredibly popular with galleries and the press. There had never been anyone quite like him in the world of golf. It's probably safe to say that, with the exceptions of Arnold Palmer and Sam Snead, no other great golfers have ever truly enjoyed the game as much just for the game's sake. Indeed, if professional golf were to dry up and go away tomorrow, on the day after tomorrow Lee Trevino would surface somewhere playing the game just for the sheer joy of playing.

●

*M*y first wife, Claudia, never cared all that much for trophies, but when she saw the sculpture of Ben Hogan's hands on the Hogan Trophy [given to the player who comes back from serious injury or illness] she said that was the one trophy she wanted in the house.

" 'Are you crazy?' I said. 'Do you know what you have to do to win that? You have to do what Hogan did. You have to get hit by a bus.' "

*W*hen Lee Trevino won the 1971 British Open at Royal Birkdale he was told that it was something of a tradition for the champion to give a bit of his check to a local Catholic orphanage.

Trevino agreed to give $1,500 on the condition that the nuns from the orphanage come to the nearby Kingsway Casino and share a glass of champagne with him. The nuns agreed, although none of them had ever had a drink, much less been in a casino.

In the end Trevino was so moved by it all that he auctioned off the clubs he had used to win the Open and donated the proceeds—another $1,500—to the kids.

●

I grew up playing on a public course in Dallas called Tennison Park," Trevino recalls. "It was so tough out there that people would skip a stretch of holes away from the clubhouse for fear of getting robbed.

"One day these two guys are out there playing a match, and the bets are flying fast and furious. One guy's out $1,000. Just then, these two robbers pop out of the trees with guns.

" 'Here,' the guy who was losing said, handing over $1,000 to his friend. 'We're even.' "

●

*W*hen the United States Ryder Cup team traveled to Walton Heath in England for the 1981 matches, Trevino was paired with Jerry Pate, who had won the U.S.

Amateur, the U.S. Open, and The Players Championship. Pate was a beautiful player who hadn't had much match play experience. Trevino had the solution to that problem.

"Jerry, I'll pick the clubs for you, and you just hit them," Trevino told him. "Don't worry about thinking or trying anything fancy. I'll do the thinking and the fancy stuff for both of us."

•

GENE TUNNEY

*P*aul Runyan, the two-time PGA Champion and former leading money winner on tour has a memorable story about the former heavyweight champion:

"One year I was playing in the Seminole Pro-Am, which was quite a big event on our winter circuit," the diminutive Runyan recalled. "On the first hole my partner hit his drive a full 310 yards and then hit his approach eighteen inches from the hole. I'm thinking about my incredible good fortune. Nobody even hinted the man could play like this. Of course, as soon as I began thinking like that he tapped his gimme putt twenty feet past the hole. That is how I met Mr. Gene Tunney, the heavyweight champion of the world."

JOE TURNESA

*T*he Turnesa brothers—Joe, Jim, Mike and Willie—enjoyed wonderful successes in golf in both the amateur and professional ranks. But while their father, a greenskeeper, was proud of them, he didn't let it go to his head.

"Mr. Turnesa, Joe's leading the Open!" said a club member when a news report from the 1926 Open came over the radio.

"Why shouldn't he?" said Mr. Turnesa, not looking up from his work. "All he's ever done is play golf."

HARRY VARDON

*E*ngland's Harry Vardon won a record six British Opens and a U.S. Open and is generally credited with developing the Vardon, or overlapping, grip, the most popular grip in the game.

Vardon suffered an attack of tuberculosis following his British Open win in 1903 but remained a factor in major championships into his fifties. He finished second to his great rival, Ted Ray, in the 1920 U.S. Open at Inverness Country Club in Toledo when he missed a three-foot putt on the 72nd hole.

One of the members asked Vardon how a player as great as he could manage to miss such a short putt. Vardon decided to give the gentleman a taste of championship pressure.

Vardon bet the man $100 that one week from that day the member couldn't make the identical putt Vardon had missed. For good measure, Vardon told the man he could practice the putt all week.

The man snapped up the bet. The news made all the papers. A huge crowd showed up at the appointed hour. The member missed the putt. Badly. Vardon collected his $100, and hackers everywhere got a lesson in just what tournament pressure is really like.

Vardon was paired with Bob Jones in the 1920 U.S. Open at Inverness. Both went out in opening round 76s. In the second round Jones chose to play a pitch-and-run into the 7th hole but skulled the shot, sending it racing over the green and into the back bunker. From there, the best he could salvage was a bogey 5. As he walked to the next tee, he sought to ease the tension by speaking with Vardon, who had remained speechless until that point in the round.

"Mr. Vardon, did you ever see a worse shot than that?" Jones asked.

"No," he said. Period.

●

Vardon was a supremely skillful ball-striker, said to be as good as anyone who ever played.

Vardon toured America in 1900, at a time when he was at the height of his skills and the game was beginning to grow in the States. In Boston he agreed to do a series of exhibitions at Jordan Marsh, the huge department store. Even though he was paid a great deal of money for his efforts, he thought standing around hitting balls into a net was somewhat degrading, not to mention boring. To make things more interesting, he concentrated on trying to hit a valve handle on a fire extinguisher that stuck through the netting he hit into. The handle was about the size of a silver dollar, but Vardon hit it with such stunning regularity that the store manager begged him to stop for fear of setting off a flood.

During this visit he played a match against H. M. Harriman, the reigning U.S. Amateur Champion, and Findlay S. Douglas, who had held the title the previous year and finished as runner-up to Harriman in his defense. Vardon played their best ball and won the 36-hole match 9 and 8.

KEN VENTURI

"When I look back on my career, I was really lucky. I learned to play from Nelson and Hogan, which is like learning to paint from Michelangelo and Leonardo. How's it get better than that?"

—Ken Venturi

*I*n the years that I've known Ken Venturi we've done a book and a couple of videos together, played a lot of golf, and done a fair amount of just hanging around. It's impossible to figure out which time was most enjoyable or best spent.

People sometimes ask if Ken can still play, and the answer is definitely, although to go out and play the Senior Tour at the level he'd demand of himself would force him to quit CBS.

People also ask if he's a good teacher, and the answer is one of the best. I've seen him twice turn down offers of blank checks to work with players, largely because he knew he didn't have the time—or they didn't have the real desire—to get as good as they hoped . . . and he's never been one to just take the money. In an era when some teachers have come to resemble movie stars in their insatiable desire for publicity, he's helped a hell of a lot more players than he's ever received credit for.

Different people will leave different legacies to the game. In one sense, Ken's legacy will not be the tournaments he won or the beauty of his play. Injuries took care of that. But it will be the courage he brought to golf and what he's given back to the game in hundreds of ways, both large and small.

●

*F*ew stories in any sport are as moving as Ken Venturi's. One of the top amateurs in the 1950s, he turned pro and quickly became one of the tour's genuine superstars. But a series of injuries sent him into a despairing collapse, to the point where he came close to quitting golf altogether.

As his frustrations multiplied, Venturi, at age thirty-three, felt he had reached the absolute bottom. One evening he went to the basement of his house and prayed.

"I just asked God please not to let me go out this way," he recalled. "It wasn't that I had to win. I had gotten past that. But I needed to prove that I could still play, that I hadn't wasted everything I once had."

Venturi made a vow. He would work hard to get himself and his game back into shape for one more season; 1964 would be his make-or-break year. The year did not begin with much promise, and by the time June came around this enormously proud man was reduced to begging sponsors for exemptions into their events.

"I called Bill Jennings, who ran the Thunderbird Tournament in Westchester County. I felt my game was finally coming around, and I pleaded with him for a spot in his tournament. He had one left and gave it to me."

Venturi, who had struggled all year, played his way into contention. As he was leaving the clubhouse for the final round, he overheard a father telling his son, "That's Ken

Venturi. He used to be one of the great players."

Venturi made a promise to himself. He would prove the man wrong. When he came to the 16th hole, a long dangerous par 3, he considered playing the safe shot rather than attacking the pin and risking a big number. He thought about that man and his son. Then he thought about one other thing.

"I told myself that this was it," Venturi recalls. "If I backed off now I knew I would be backing off for the rest of my life."

Venturi pulled out a 3-iron and rifled it at the flag. The shot was perfect, and while he missed his birdie putt, he had proven something to himself and to all those around him. His third-place finish set the stage for one of the greatest triumphs in golf history: Ken Venturi's win in the 1964 U.S. Open.

When Venturi arrived in suburban Washington, D.C., for the Open, he sought out a Catholic church. Alone in the church that evening he prayed, again asking God to give him the confidence and strength that he needed. He also asked for some sort of sign that his prayers had been heard.

That sign emerged on the eve of Saturday's final two rounds, when he received a letter from a friend, Father Frank Murray. The letter began:

"Dear Ken:
    For you to become the 1964 U.S. Open Champion would be one of the greatest things that ever happened during the year in the United States.
    There are so many people in this country and in the world that need the encouragement and inspiration that your winning would give them.
    Most people are in the midst of struggle. If not with their jobs, then it's their family life, or their health, or their drinking, or their frustrations. For

many there is the constant temptation to give up and to quit trying. Life seems too much, and the demands too great. . . ."

Saturday's thirty-six-hole final round was brutal. The heat and humidity hovered near 105 degrees. Venturi, paired with young Raymond Floyd, went out in 30 strokes. On the 14th hole his body began to tremble from the intense heat. On 17, as he stood over a two-foot par putt, he hallucinated, seeing three holes. He putted for the middle hole and missed. Another bogey on 18 left him with a 66 and a three-round total of 208.

In the clubhouse between rounds, he was advised by a physician not to play the second eighteen. "Ken," said Dr. John Knowles, "if you go out there you could very easily die."

"Doc," said Venturi, "I'm already dying. I've got no place else to go."

Venturi went out and gamely fought on, playing largely on instinct and emotion. He went out in 35, and as he stood on the 10th tee Joseph C. Dey, the director of the United States Golf Association, told him he had the lead.

"There's a scoreboard over there if you're interested, Ken," said Dey.

"I'm not interested," Venturi said. "I can't change what's up there, and I can't control what the other guys are doing. One shot at a time is all that interests me."

As he left the 17th tee, Venturi knew he still had the lead, but again he was on the verge of collapse.

"Joe, you can put two strokes on me for slow play, but I've just got to walk slowly," he told Dey.

"Ken, it's all downhill to the 18th green," said Dey. "Now how about holding your chin up, so when you come in as a champion you'll look like one."

When he sank the winning putt on the 72nd hole, Venturi threw his arms into the air and then collapsed in tears. "My God," he said softly. "I've won the Open."

A few minutes later, in the scorer's tent, he tried to check his score, knowing that a mistake could cost him the Open. Fear swept over him as he was unable to focus on his card. Then he heard a voice from over his shoulder.

"Sign it, Ken. It's fine," said Dey, who had walked every step of the final round with Venturi, the new U.S. Open Champion and a man who had come back from the dead.

●

*A*s one of the nation's top amateurs in the 1950s, Ken came under the wing of Eddie Lowery, a prominent San Francisco businessman who as a boy had caddied for Francis Ouimet in his U.S. Open victory. Lowery was well connected in the golf world and wanted to help Venturi develop his game. He arranged for Venturi to work with his friend Byron Nelson, but first he wanted to make sure that Venturi's native confidence didn't spill over into arrogance.

"Ken, do you have a dictionary at home?" asked Lowery.

"Sure," said Venturi.

"Good, because I want you to go home and look up the meaning of the word *humility*, because you don't have a bit of it," said Lowery.

●

*I*t was fitting that Nelson captained the only Ryder Cup team Ken Venturi played on in his injury-ravaged career. The 1965 matches were played at Royal Birkdale in Southport, England. While the Americans would go on to win 19½-12½, a turning point came in an alternate-shot match that paired Venturi and Tony Lema against Neil Coles and Brian Barnes.

On a par 5 hole late in the match, Lema hooked his second shot behind a bunker, leaving Venturi a delicate pitch off a downhill lie to a pin cut just over the bunker.

"I'm afraid things don't look very good for your side," Prime Minister Harold Wilson said to Nelson. "I don't favor your man Venturi's chances with this shot. I believe the match may go even here."

"That may be, Mr. Wilson," replied Nelson. "But I've got ten men on this team, and if I had to pick one man to play this shot for me, it's the man playing the shot right now."

Venturi's pitch finished stiff to the pin.

"My, Mr. Nelson," said Wilson. "You do know your men, don't you?"

●

Venturi might have gone on to a career in baseball if he hadn't stuttered as a youngster. He was so ashamed of his affliction that he took up golf, where he could be by himself.

He learned to play at San Francisco's Harding Park, a public course, where he would offer commentary about his round, struggling to overcome his stutter.

"It was a funny thing, but looking back, the only tournament I'd ever imagine myself winning was the Open," he recalls. "I'd always say, 'This is Ken Venturi's putt for the U.S. Open' or 'Here's Ken Venturi on the final tee, needing a good drive to set up his win in the Open.'"

In another irony, his last win, the 1966 Lucky International, came at Harding Park, before the people who had loved him and lived through his highs and lows.

"I had always prayed that I could go out like a champion," he recalls. "Winning at Harding Park and beating Arnold down the stretch let me do just that."

TOM WATSON

"A fine golfer has only one fine thing, and that's his fine golf, and if he ever forgets it, he's a fool. Tom Watson never forgets."

—Byron Nelson

*W*hat is there, really, to say about Tom Watson? That he was the dominant player of his generation? That he overcame the mindless label "Choker" to challenge—and beat—Jack Nicklaus head-to-head in the battles that matter the most—the Majors? That when, at the top of his game, he mysteriously stopped winning, he never complained and never made excuses? And never gave up?

All of that, to be sure—but maybe more than anything else, Tom Watson played the game with uncompromising character and, for a time, singular distinction.

Have we seen the last of Tom Watson? No. In fact, we may not have seen the best yet.

●

*B*y 1977 Tom Watson had already established himself as a premier player, having won his first British Open and a couple of tour events. But in that year he became a

209

player for history. He arrived at Turnberry and the British Open with four tour wins in 1977, including his first of two Masters.

The championship quickly evolved into a two-man battle, as Watson and Nicklaus opened with identical rounds of 68-70-65. In the final round Nicklaus took a two-shot lead with just six holes to play. So great was the drama that it attracted the highest possible compliment from their fellow players, who broke with tradition and came out on the course to watch the closing holes in person. And what a show they saw.

Watson drew even on the par 3 15th, when he ran in a sixty-footer from off the green.

As they stood on the 16th tee waiting for the huge galleries to clear, Watson turned to Nicklaus and said, "This is what it's all about, isn't it?"

"You bet it is,"said Nicklaus, smiling.

The 16th was halved with pars. On 17, a 500-yard par 5, Watson stung a courageous 3-iron to within twenty feet for his eagle. Nicklaus flinched. His 4-iron approach missed the green, leaving a particularly nasty chip, which he got to within four feet. When he missed the putt, Tom Watson took the lead for the first time in the championship.

On 18 Watson drilled a 1-iron into the heart of the fairway then hit a 7-iron to within two feet. Nicklaus, being Nicklaus, rallied from a poor drive to hit his approach to forty feet and then made the putt.

It was then that Tom Watson became truly and fully Tom Watson—by making his birdie putt for his second British Open.

In the end it was left to Nicklaus to pay him the ultimate compliment.

"I threw my best at him," said Nicklaus. "I gave him everything I had. I just couldn't shake him."

"I want to get to the day when everything will fall into place; when everything makes sense, when every swing is with confidence, and every shot is exactly what I want. I know it can be done. I've been close enough to smell it a few times, but I'd like to touch it, to feel it. I know it's been touched. Hogan touched it. Byron touched it. I want to touch it. Then, I think I'd be satisfied. Then, and only then, I think I could walk away from the game truly satisfied."

—Tom Watson

●

I n 1980, the year Tom won the British Open at Muirfield, we were having dinner and a member came by and gave me four old hickory-shafted clubs and some gutta-percha balls," recalls Ben Crenshaw. "Tom and I went out and played the 10th and 18th holes. We both made 5s on 10, and Tom beat me with a 4 on 18. As we were finishing, Paddy Hammer, the club secretary, came out and got all over us. He was really upset and ordered us off the course, telling us that we should be ashamed of ourselves and that we should know better. I don't think either of us had been yelled at like that since we were kids."

TOM WEISKOPF

*T*om Weiskopf is one of the true talents and true characters of the game. Tall, elegant, and outspoken.

In the past few years Weiskopf has severely reduced his tournament play in favor of his golf course architecture with Jay Morrish. He is one of the few player-architects to be almost uniformly praised for both his work and his devotion to the job. But when he does play he remains something to behold. His swing is still a thing of beauty, and he can still control the ball magnificently. After seeing him play, people invariably wonder why he's all but hung up his spikes. One theory is that he got tired of seeing lesser players win tournaments. Another is that he got tired of the selfishness that tournament golf requires, electing the teamwork that his partnership with Morrish offered.

Whatever his reasons, if Tom Weiskopf never quite lived up to other people's expectations for his career, he remains true to himself to this day—a man who marches to the beat of his own drummer.

*F*ollowing a round in the 1980 British Open at Muir-field, Tom Weiskopf and his wife, Jeanne, were with some friends in the Greywalls hotel watching the BBC's Open coverage.

"I was criticizing the BBC, and I noticed that Jeanne kept motioning me to be quiet, but she was being very subtle about it," he recalls. "Finally, this woman who was with us got up and left.

"Tom, do you know who that woman is?" she asked me.

"I give up. She's the Queen of England," I said.

"Close—she's her sister, Princess Margaret."

Well, I felt pretty bad, and when the princess came back I went out of my way to be polite. We were having a very nice conversation, and she mentioned that her father loved to play golf.

"That's nice," I said. "What did your father do?"

"He was the King of England," said the princess.

Jeanne was horrified, but the princess took it pretty well. Heck, she still tells the story all the time.

●

*L*ike may top golfers—and others in public life—the real Tom Weiskopf was often at odds with the public's and press's perceptions. Many would be surprised to learn, for example, that as he stood in the 18th fairway at Troon after hitting his final approach and insuring his win in the 1973 British Open, he turned to his caddie, Albert Fyles, with tears in his eyes and said, "There's one man I'd dearly love to be in those stands, Albert—my dad." His father had died earlier that year.

*J*ack [Nicklaus] and I always used to go over and play our practice rounds together beginning the week before the British Open," Weiskopf recalls. "At Carnoustie in 1975 we went out one evening after dinner, which was fairly normal since it stays light for so long. We were on the second green when we heard Australian Jack Newton [who would lose to Tom Watson in a play-off] and [Irish professional] John O'Leary calling to us from the tee. When they caught up with us, Jack Newton said they wanted to challenge us to a game. Nicklaus made it a practice of not playing for anything during practice rounds, because he was never shooting for a score but trying to fit his game to how the course would play that week.

"Now, you have to keep in mind that even though we were playing in the evening, we had a gallery of several hundred people. Newton kept badgering Jack, saying things like 'You are supposed to be the two best players in the world but you're afraid to play us' and so on. On the 3rd hole Newton made a birdie; then he ran in a forty-footer for another birdie on 4. When it went in he looked over at Jack and asked if we wanted a press. Now, until that point we hadn't even said we wanted a game, but Nicklaus looked over at Newton with a look I don't ever think I'd seen before or since. He said, 'Jack, we're not two down yet.' With that, he ran in a ten-footer for birdie.

"All of a sudden, the game was on. We decided to play $10 automatic one-downs. On the fifth tee Jack took me aside and put those steely blues on me. 'Tom,' he said, 'if you've ever really tried I want you to try now. I want to bury these guys.' He was scary.

"I've never seen Jack quite as intense as he was that night. Between us we made twelve birdies and an eagle over the next fourteen holes. And that doesn't count what happened on the 8th hole, which is one of the hardest par 3s you'll ever see.

"Nicklaus hit first and got his ball on the green. The pin was hidden behind some mounds, and I shot right at the flag. We couldn't see it land, but the gallery applauded politely, so we figured it was safe. When we reached the green, we could see three balls, but not mine. Finally Nicklaus went up and found my ball in the hole.

" 'Can you believe it?' he said. 'You made a hole-in-one and nobody said anything?'

"With that, he walked over to these two old Scots sitting on their shooting sticks.

" 'Were you there when Tom hit his shot?' Jack asked them.

" 'Aye, Jack,' one of them replied.

" 'Did you realize it went in the hole?'

" 'Aye, Jack,' the guy said. 'But isn't it only practice?' "

●

The relationship between Tom Weiskopf and Jack Nicklaus is one of the most complex in golf. Tom is two years younger than Jack and played in his shadow as a teenager growing up in Ohio, as a student at Ohio State, and on tour. Nicklaus respects Weiskopf's enormous talent but on occasion has been mystified by Weiskopf's single-minded insistence on doing things his own way.

One such occasion occurred at the 1979 British Open at Royal Lytham when Weiskopf, at the end of a frustrating round, hit his eighty-yard approach to the 16th green with a putter and then repaired to the Clifton Arms Hotel to meet some friends. A while later Nicklaus sought out Weiskopf and asked him if the story was true.

"Well, Jack, I did want to keep the ball under the wind," said Weiskopf, to laughter from his friends.

Nicklaus simply looked Weiskopf in the eye, sadly shook his head, and left.

*F*or better or worse, Tom Weiskopf is one of those people who just seem to have weird—or funny—things happen to them. Take his visit to St. Andrews in 1974. He had won the British Open the previous year at Troon and came to St. Andrews with three friends for a round at the Old Course.

He went to the starter's shed, paid his greens fee, and asked if he might have a couple of extra scorecards and pencils for his friends.

"No sir," said the starter. "There'll be one scorecard and one pencil per group."

With that, Weiskopf walked to the back of the tee box to hit his drive from where the championship markers would ordinarily be placed. Before he could even take a practice swing, the starter came racing out of his shed.

"Sir, and you'll be playing from the public markers, thank you," he admonished the reigning Open champion.

●

*T*om Weiskopf's first check on tour came in the 1964 Western Open, when he won $487.50. Every year since he has written a check for that amount to the Western Golf Association's Evans Caddie Scholarship Fund.

●

*O*ver the course of his career, Weiskopf has also written out a few checks for fines levied by PGA Tour Commissioner Deane Beman, with whom he's had a running battle of sorts.

In 1974 Beman told Weiskopf he was fining him $500

for walking off the course during the PGA Championship at Tanglewood Golf Club.

"Is that the best you can do?" Weiskopf asked.

Beman's answer was to double the fine to $1,000.

●

JOYCE WETHERED

*J*oyce Wethered, now Lady Heathcoat-Amory, is arguably the greatest female golfer in British history and, some would say, in all of golf. She won, among other titles, four British Women's Championships and five English Women's Championships.

Like every outstanding player, she was graced with both athletic skill and an almost superhuman ability to concentrate, as Cecil Leitch, one of her greatest rivals explains:

"As Miss Wethered was preparing to putt for the win and the title of 1920 English champion, a long train suddenly rattled by, making the most horrible noise. She appeared quite unbothered by the train, in fact, appeared almost in a trance, quite unconscious of any of her immediate surroundings. Later, I asked her if the train had not bothered her. She replied by asking, 'What train?' Remarkable. Utterly remarkable."

BABE ZAHARIAS

*A*ny list of great athletes, male or female, must include Babe Zaharias. She won two gold medals and a silver in the 1932 Olympics and then set her sights on golf. After winning both the British and U.S. Women's Amateurs, she turned pro, becoming one of the founding members of the LPGA. She was one of the dominant players in the game, winning three U.S. Women's Opens before her death from cancer in 1956 at age forty-one.

●

*I*n my rookie year I was paired with Babe in a four-ball tournament," recalls Peggy Kirk Bell, who would go on to become both a top touring pro and a teacher. "I was naturally very nervous, and I told Babe that I'd do my best and hoped I could help her enough so we could win.

" 'Win!' she roared, 'of course we'll win. We can't lose. I can beat any two of these girls on my own. You just come along and have a good time.' "

*B*abe Zaharias won the U.S. Women's Open in both 1948 and 1950 but was hospitalized for cancer in 1953, when she underwent a colostomy. In 1954 a weakened Zaharias came back to win her third Women's Open at Salem Country Club. Her recovery, however, was short lived. By 1956 she was back in a Galveston, Texas hospital.

"She was very weak, but she never lost her love for the game," recalls her friend Betty Dodd. "On a good day, she would go down to the beach and hit a few very gentle wedge shots into the surf, then slowly return to her room."

She died on September 27, 1956.

INDEX